CW00351683

The Church Explorer's Handbook

This book is dedicated to the many small communities, rural and urban, who keep their churches open and well cared for and their churchyards well managed but not over-tidy. It is also dedicated to the thousands of people who go driving, cycling and walking around Britain in search of nothing in particular, yet manage to discover and explore these wonderful buildings.

'. . . a new general introduction to the fascinations of the English parish church is long overdue. This one . . . is arguably the most erudite.'

Dr Julian Litten in The Church Times

Our churches are our history shown
In wood and glass and iron and stone

John Betjeman

The Church Explorer's Handbook

A Guide to Looking at Churches and their Contents

Clive Fewins

CANTERBURY
PRESS

Norwich

© Open Churches Trust 2005

First published in 2005 by the Canterbury Press Norwich
(a publishing imprint of Hymns Ancient & Modern Limited,
a registered charity)
13A Hellesdon Park Road
Norwich, Norfolk, NR6 5DR

www.canterburypress.co.uk

Fifth impression 2012

The publisher acknowledges with thanks permission to
use illustrations from the poster 'The English Parish
Church' © The Book on the Wall Company.

British Library Cataloguing in Publication data

A catalogue record for this book is available
from the British Library

ISBN 978-1-85311-622-3

Typeset by Regent Typesetting, London
Printed and bound by
MPG Books Ltd, Bodmin, Cornwall

Contents

Appendices

Foreword
By Andrew Lloyd Webber

When I started the Open Churches Trust over ten years ago, it was in the hope that its work would act as a catalyst to encourage like-minded people and institutions to start working to the same end.

Little did I know that within a decade not only having an open church would be back in vogue but that over 30 million people a year would be visiting places of worship.

In support of this remarkable transformation of attitudes, the Trust is publishing a pocket-sized book, *The Church Explorer's Handbook*, to enable future millions of visitors to understand and enjoy what they see.

The author, Clive Fewins, published some years ago a book for young people called *Be a Church Detective* which in an exciting way lures young visitors to look for the interesting parts of a church and understand why they are there in the first place. It has proved to be an extremely popular publication just re-published.

The Church Explorer's Handbook fulfils a similar role for adults. Every facet is dealt with in an easily readable way with plenty of references to where you will find examples of the features described.

The publishers, Canterbury Press, have produced a very complete reference book, designed to be in your Barbour pocket or car pocket so that it is always handy when heading for any of our 16,000 parish churches.

I strongly recommend this excellent publication, which fills a huge gap in our understanding of one of the most amazing collections of buildings in the world, which are increasingly becoming accessible.

Acknowledgements

The author is hugely indebted to Roy Tricker, co-author of the excellent *County Guide to English Parish Churches*, for his unstinting help and constant encouragement during this project. The author also acknowledges with gratitude the invaluable assistance of the following people in the preparation of this book: Adam Gurdon, Christina Robertson, Edward Martin, Hilary Lees, Ian Smith, Jane Bingham, John Vigar, 'Lyn Stilgoe, Martin Stuchfield, Martin Trowell, Michael O'Dougan, Nicholas Gendle, Patrick Powers, Ron Foster, Rosemary Watts and Sandy Marchant.

None of this would have been possible without the constant and long-suffering support of a patient wife, who accompanied me with little complaint around scores of churches all over England and Wales in all weathers.

Clive Fewins

Introduction

This handbook is an aid to people who like to go out and explore churches, and to enthuse those who think they might like to do so. It tries to explain the many attractions of church exploring and attempts to encourage people to take up this pastime.

It is also designed to help you spot the interesting features in and around any church, and so includes many lists of the places where these things can be seen. The lists are not exhaustive, but they home in on particular features and where they can be found. They supplement the gazeteer in Appendices 1 and 2, which give a selection of more than 1,000 churches considered worth making a detour to visit in all the English and Welsh counties and in Scotland.

The idea is that by keeping this book with you when you are on your travels, by car or on foot or bicycle, you will be in a better position to explore the churches that you discover on your route. It should also prove useful to refer to when planning your trip; and on returning home, as a means of finding out more about church buildings in general.

The book also helps you to take a look at the churchyard (if there is one) and stresses that you will only gain the maximum enjoyment from a church if your visit also results in a greater understanding of its setting and the community it serves.

It is quite hard to get to grips with the fact that there are some 16,000 parish churches to be explored in England and Wales. As every one is different, this means that there is a huge variety. And as there is something of interest to someone in every church, whatever its size, age, setting or architectural style, it underlines the sheer scope of church exploring as a hobby.

The book also tries to make the point that you do not have to be an 'expert' in order to enjoy exploring churches. While it is written by a practising Anglican it goes out of its way to avoid proselytizing: it is a book about church buildings, not a book about the Christian faith.

With people's increasing mobility and leisure time, church exploring as a hobby has gained hugely in popularity in the last 20–30 years. The 10,000 or so medieval churches are all treasure houses in one way or another. They are full of interest for people with an enquiring mind, on many fronts – art, memorials, woodwork, stained glass, sculpture – or any combination of them, to name but a few.

It is often said that if you want to learn about a place you should make the parish church your first port of call. One good reason for this is that it is likely to be the oldest building in the locality that is regularly open to the general public.

In many ways church exploring encompasses the best bits of many other hobbies. It is outdoors, it involves a certain amount of exercise, it gets the mind working, and it gets you to places where you might well not normally go. It is also a hobby that satisfies anyone with a strong interest in local history – or simply in how a community has lived over 1,000 or so years

However dark and dreary and unappealing the poky and unloved wayside church you happen upon, discovering why it is there and understanding its history and structure is like unravelling a complex detective story. If this kind of church is of interest, then no wonder tourists and other visitors flock to see the great medieval wonders of the Cotswolds and East Anglia!

Churches are not museums, nor monuments – ancient or modern – and they can be entered free of charge. There is no subscription needed to be a church explorer, but please do not forget that every church welcomes a contribution towards its maintenance.

If you think it would be fun to confine your interest in churches to visiting all the medieval churches in England and Wales you will still have to work extremely hard. Someone once calculated that if you were able to start church exploring soon after birth and see 100 fresh churches every year, then if you live to be 100 you should just about manage to see them all!

Sir John Betjeman, who in the 1950s opened the eyes of many to the glories of our parish churches and of the enjoyment to be gained exploring them, used to say there was no need to be dull when either writing or speaking about churches.

The intention of this book is to fire your enthusiasm and add to your knowledge, but never – it is hoped – to be dull.

How to Use This Book

This is a handbook. It is designed as a book to which you can refer and which can be dipped into, not read whole. If you find a topic of interest half way through and feel lost, then look at the table of contents and go back to the point where the information you need is provided. For this reason you may, if you wish, skip the rather long section which deals with identifying the basic forms of church architecture over the centuries, and come back to it when you feel the need for further explanation.

At certain points, a subject may of necessity be treated rather briefly, and further reading and reference is provided in Appendix 4 'Further Reading'.

The book is designed to be kept in your jacket pocket when on your feet, or in a car door or glove compartment (or wrapped in a plastic bag on your bicycle carrier!) when you are on the move.

For motorists, one of the principal arguments in the handbook is that road travel in this country is much enhanced by allowing an extra couple of hours, planning a route that (partially at least) uses secondary roads, and 'taking in' a church or two on your journey. It argues that, in true 'Renaissance' fashion, you will be the better for that experience.

It is – quite specifically – *not* a 'religious' book. It is designed to appeal to people of any faith or of no faith at all. You don't have to be 'churchy' to enjoy exploring churches.

Although most of the churches mentioned are necessarily Anglican, there is a smattering in Appendix 2 and throughout the book of Roman Catholic and Nonconformist churches.

This book is intended to support and reinforce the efforts of the Open Churches Trust, a charity dedicated to ensuring that as many as possible of the best parish churches and other places of worship are kept open for the public to enjoy. Its ultimate aim is that all should be open, so that anyone can wander in and out at will. You can read more about its work on pages 246–7.

Sadly not all churches are left open during the daytime and gaining entry can sometimes be a problem. If a church is closed and there is no note at the door telling you where the key can be borrowed from, there are various other things you can do in advance. This subject is dealt with in the chapter on Access.

Unlike other hobbies, church exploring needs very little equipment. Church explorers should always carry a pair of stout shoes that will withstand uneven churchyard surfaces and long wet grass. A pair of binoculars might also be useful for looking up at architectural details. A torch can also be of help in looking at odd corners of dimly lit churches. Other good advice from seasoned church explorers is take a good look all round the outside of a church before entering. If it is closed then you have even better reasons for heeding the advice given in Part 1! It is also wise not to attempt to do too much in a day. If you rush through too many churches then you will miss things and this might well prove a cause for regret. Three or four churches in a day usually proves quite enough for most people – especially if the churches are some miles apart.

Happy church exploring!

PART 1

The Church from the Outside

1

A Walk around the Outside

I have a good eye, uncle: I can see a church by daylight
Shakespeare

Every church is different, which is one reason why church exploring is such a fascinating pastime. With a little practice you can soon spot all sorts of interesting things without entering a church, so exploring churches can be fun even if the church you are visiting is locked and you can't get inside.

The setting

The first question to ask yourself is why is the church *there*? The answer, of course, is as a place of worship and to make a statement about the Christian faith. But physical location is a fascinating subject when you get into it.

St Michael, Duntisbourne Rouse, Gloucestershire, an archetypal small English parish church. There is Anglo-Saxon work and an interesting saddleback tower.

Anglo-Saxon work incorporated into an exterior buttress of a Cotswold parish church.

It is a good idea to stand back and view the building as a whole from the outside. By standing back and just looking you will probably be able to see quite plainly where the church has been extended in length, and possibly also in width and height, over the centuries. This will help you with your exploration once you get inside. Most ancient parish churches are a combination of work from many different periods, which is one reason why people particularly interested in architecture gain a great kick from unravelling the mysteries of old parish churches.

Perhaps the church you are standing beside is not in the centre of its community, but at the end of a farm track on the edge of the village.

Ask yourself why it is isolated. You may gain some clues by simply walking around and looking for indicators such as the lie of the land. By asking around you may be able to find out if it is isolated because there was an adjacent great house which has long since vanished – perhaps due to fire or to a Civil War battle or other military action, or some other disaster.

Or is it possibly the only building left standing from a former settlement that moved for some reason? It could have been the Black Death or another bout of plague, or the whims of a wealthy landowner, or some other reason. There is, for example, no trace of the great mansion that stood beside the fine Perpendicular church at Hillesden, in Buckinghamshire, which was destroyed in

Knowlton, Dorset: the ruins of an ancient flint-and-stone church lie in the centre of three Neolithic henge monuments.

the Civil War. At Wharram Percy in the Yorkshire Wolds the church still stands, ruined and abandoned. In 1348–49 the village was badly affected by the Black Death, but the village was not abandoned until shortly after 1500. St Martin's church continued to be used for another 400 years, but attendances tailed off greatly when a new church was built in a nearby village in 1870. St Martin's fell into disrepair and was abandoned after the last service was held there in 1949. The tower collapsed in December 1959.

At Stoke Charity in Hampshire the small church of St Mary and St Michael – there is still an active congregation – stands alone in the middle of a field surrounded by odd bumps in the ground – all that is left of a long-lost mansion that was demolished in 1730.

At Binham in Norfolk the parish church is all that remains of a huge Benedictine priory which was vastly reduced in the reign of Henry VIII during the Dissolution of the Monasteries (see page 81).

At Wheatfield in Oxfordshire in the mid-eighteenth century the local landowner razed the village to the ground and rehoused all the locals so he could create a park around his mansion. The church became his private chapel.

Not far away near Oxford in the 1760s the entire village of Nuneham Courtenay, including the church, was demolished by the landowner, Lord Harcourt, to make way for his new land-

*Stoke Charity, Hampshire: the church of St Mary and
St Michael, which dates mainly from the 12th and 13th
centuries, stands alone in a field. The adjoining mansion was
demolished in 1730.*

scaped park. A replacement church was built in Classical style in
the park. The episode inspired the poet Oliver Goldsmith to write
his famous poem 'The Deserted Village'.

Sometimes we are not sure why the great mansion disappeared,
as in the case of Snarford in Lincolnshire.

There are many similar examples throughout the country
where dramatic circumstances – depopulation is another – have
left a church isolated. However, Nuneham Courtenay is also a
good example of how many churches grew up as part of estates.

Church and manor house close together

Many ancient churches were built on Anglo-Saxon estates or by
Norman manorial lords, primarily as private chapels to serve
their new settlements. In medieval times the lord of the manor
was usually responsible for building the parish church, and he
frequently did so on his own land near his house.

Of course there were many changes over the years, and some of
these great estates have changed beyond recognition, or sunk
without trace beneath developing towns. The other thing to note
is that many of these 'estate' churches were drastically altered or
rebuilt in the seventeenth and eighteenth centuries. This was the

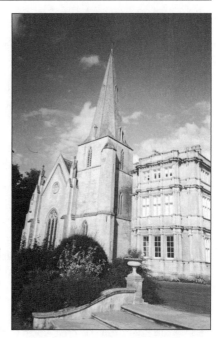

Church and adjoining manor house, Sherborne, Gloucestershire.

period when architecture in the Classical style was fashionable and the lord of the manor wished to see a Greek-style temple rather than a medieval Gothic church in his grounds.

There are hundreds of these so-called 'manorial' churches in various styles to be seen all over England. In fact it is no exaggeration to say that the majority of parish churches probably came into being in this way.

Some readily identifiable and particularly interesting examples of manorial churches:

Bedfordshire: Melchbourne
Berkshire: Englefield, Hamstead Marshall
Buckinghamshire: Chicheley, Gayhurst, Middle Claydon, Thornton
Cambridgeshire: Croxton, Wimpole
Cheshire: Brereton, Cholmondeley, Gawsworth
Cornwall: Boconnoc, Lanhydrock

Derbyshire: Calke, Kedleston

Dorset: Charborough Chapel, Melbury Sampford

Durham: Seaham

Essex: Layer Marney

Gloucestershire: Dyrham, Great Barrington, Kempsford, Leonard Stanley, Notgrove, Rendcomb, Sevenhampton, Sherborne, Stowell, Whittington

Hampshire: Avington

Herefordshire: Brockhampton-by-Ross, Croft, Richards Castle

Hertfordshire: Ayot St Lawrence, Hunsdon, Knebworth, Stanstead Abbots

Kent: Horsmonden, Knowlton

Leicestershire: Nevill Holt, Staunton Harold

Lincolnshire: Belton

Norfolk: Gunton, Houghton, Stradsett

Nottinghamshire: Kelham, Holme Pierrepoint

Oxfordshire: Chastleton, Compton Beauchamp, Garford, Marcham, North Aston, Sparsholt

Rutland: Burley-on-the-Hill, Exton

Shropshire: Pitchford, Stokesay

Somerset: Brympton D'Evercy, North Cadbury, Wyke Champflower

Staffordshire: Blithfield Ingestre, Patshull

Suffolk: Dalham, Euston, Gipping Chapel, Little Glemham, Sotterley

Surrey: Albury, Ockham

Sussex: Ashburnham

Warwickshire: Astley, Coughton, Great Packington, Merevale, Wormleighton

West Midlands: Castle Bromwich

Wiltshire: Great Chatfield

Worcestershire: Elmley Castle, Shelsley Walsh, Wickhamford

Yorkshire: Burton Agnes, Hickleton, Ingleby Arncliffe, Sledmere

Old and new churches

In many cases the old church was superseded by a new building. A famous one is at Parracombe in Devon. Here the medieval church of St Petroc narrowly escaped demolition in 1878 when

New church built into ruins of the old at Walberswick, Suffolk.

the villagers decided to build a new church in a more convenient location. St Petroc's, now in the care of the Churches Conservation Trust and much visited by tourists, was saved by protesters led by the critic and Oxford Professor of Fine Art, John Ruskin.

In Dorset the old church of Holy Trinity at Bothenhampton, now a suburb of Bridport, was not so fortunate. All that remains of it is part of the medieval chancel and the tower. It was replaced by the new church built in Arts and Crafts style in 1889.

Another Arts and Crafts church – this time the famous stone and thatch All Saints at Brockhampton-by-Ross, Herefordshire – was built by Arts and Crafts architect W. R. Lethaby in 1901/2 to replace the medieval church that was then allowed to fall into ruins. It has now been converted into a private house.

In the village of Oddington, near Stow-on-the-Wold, Gloucestershire, the old village was abandoned in the early eighteenth century but the church of St Nicholas continued to be used until a church was built in the 'new' village in 1852. The old church was not restored and fell into an extremely dilapidated state until 1912, when, with help from the Society for the Protection of

A dramatic hilltop church, St Michael-of-the-Rock, Brentor, Devon. Access is only on foot.

Ancient Buildings, the process of restoration began. Today it is still in use.

Hilltop churches

If you visit an ancient church on top of a hill then it is always a little bit more dramatic – especially if you end up outside the remote St Michael-of-the-Rock at Brentor, on the western edge of Dartmoor in Devon, which is only accessible on foot.

This tiny church is used for regular worship for only six months of the year yet it receives thousands of visitors. There are no elements of huge architectural merit, no relics, no high-quality furnishings, and yet most people would describe it as a sacred site. Perhaps it is because, like Knowlton in Dorset, Edlesborough in Buckinghamshire, Avebury in Wiltshire, St Issey in Cornwall, Wickham St Paul in Essex, and many others, it also stands on a site where men have worshipped one god or another since pre-historic times.

A number of hilltop churches are sited on ancient burial mounds. The most famous of them in England is the ruined tower of the dramatically sited medieval chapel of St Michael that tops Glastonbury Tor in Somerset. It occupies a previous pagan defensive site. Hilltop churches are often dedicated to St Michael the Archangel and dragon slayer.

Wherever the church is – it might be beside a river, in the centre of a new housing estate or at the foot of a mountain pass in the Lake District – its site is the first point of interest to the church explorer.

A walk round the outside

The shape of the church tells you a lot. Experts often talk of churches that are 'cruciform' in shape, meaning that they take the shape of the Cross. Or that they are 'single cells', meaning that they were originally simple 'boxes' erected by the Anglo-Saxons, originally in timber and perhaps not even with a separate east-end section, what later became known as a chancel. In churches built before the Norman Conquest of 1066 you can sometimes see the equivalent of the modern chancel in the form of a narrowing at the eastern end of the building

1. Anglo-Saxon
Earlier timber church
rebuilt in stone

Chancel and
sanctuary

Nave

Arcade to
north aisle

Bell-cote

**2. Transitional Norman
– Early English**

North aisle and
chapel added

3. Early English

Nave and aisle lengthened

Tower, porch, and south
chantry chapel added

Rood and rood loft

Parclose

Chancel and tower
enlarged and south aisle
added

4. Decorated

*The development of the English parish church from the Saxon to the
Decorated phase. The plan of a typical Perpendicular church is on
pages 94–5.*

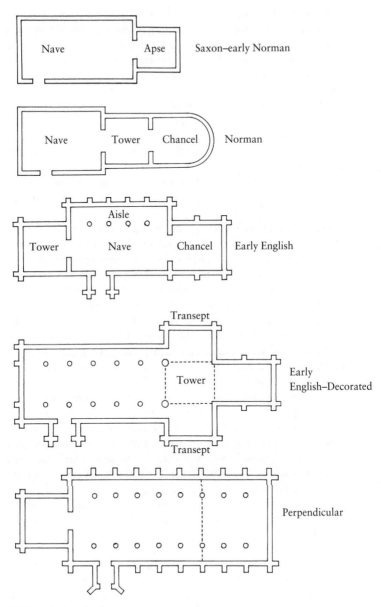

Medieval church plans.

In Norman (properly referred to as 'English Romanesque') times a tower between nave and chancel was popular. When aisles at one or both sides of the building were added this usually took place at a later stage. Likewise transepts – the projecting side-wings at right angles to the nave (the main central section of the church).

The Celtic churches – towards the end of the Dark Ages many ancient Britons became Christians – always had a square east end, but some early Norman churches followed the pattern of Roman basilicas, large roofed public buildings, and had a round east end, known as an apse.

Some church buildings are known as round churches. In this case only the nave is circular. Only five ancient ones remain (see page 88).

For many church building enthusiasts, the most interesting churches are those that fit into no precise pattern. Fortunately this is the vast majority. And it is for the simple reason that every generation has left its mark. So we are often left standing and scratching our heads, even before we enter the church, as to why the tower is situated on the north side of the church rather than being in the centre, or, as is most common, at the west end. To some this will matter little, while those of a more enquiring bent will wish to find out why. To the majority, who simply find old churches fascinating, this is simply one of the many attractions they have to offer.

In stone churches changes in masonry styles will indicate where a building has been enlarged or altered, as do straight joints. Blocked windows and doors might indicate the presence of a memorial inside. But they might indicate the presence (or past presence) of a closed or hidden chamber of some kind – perhaps an anchorite's cell. For this reason a third item of equipment the church explorer needs to keep in the car in addition to the stout shoes and binoculars is a long tape measure. This is useful for checking discrepancies between the inside and the outside of the church.

Is it usually entered by the west or south door? If so, this is fairly standard, but if it is entered by the north door this is less common. It may be because it was easier to gain access from the settlement the church served that way. Or it may be because at some stage the south porch has been turned into a vestry, or because the manor house with which the church was associated lay to the north.

What is it built of?

Why is it that there are two very different building stones in use in the walls of the church you are walking round, and that one section seems to be newer and of totally different stone from the rest of the building? The answer may be simple, and it may lie in the guidebook inside the building. But it is fun to speculate as you walk round the outside and note the different materials.

As you grow more confident you may be able to spot anomalies such as that at the church of St John at Oxborough in Norfolk. There the stone doorways in the north porch and the west window are not of the same period (Perpendicular) as the rest of the church. This is odd because porches were usually the last parts of a church to be built. The commonly held theory is that these features were moved from the ruined church half a mile away which was the parish church before the rebuilding in the fifteenth century.

St Mary, Fairford, Gloucestershire: a fine, stone Perpendicular church, and the only parish church in England to contain a complete set of late medieval glass.

Many old parish churches have a multitude of different forms of stone in their walls. When studying the outside look out for signs of old blocked doorways.

Not all churches are built of stone, of course. We know the earliest churches were built of timber. One, St Andrew, at Greensted-juxta-Ongar in Essex, has large sections of its original wooden structure surviving and is the oldest wooden church in the world.

Stone was favoured by most of the medieval church builders, but even then it was a luxury because it was difficult to extract by hand.

It is ironic that in today's technological age stone is not difficult to extract, work or transport; but it would be extremely rare to find a new church with walls faced entirely with stone, because of the cost of labour and the environmental cost of extracting stone from quarries in our increasingly protected countryside.

This alone is a good reason why we should protect, fight for and celebrate the qualities of the fabric of our ancient parish churches. These are things that all too often cannot be repeated.

For all these reasons in areas where fine freestone (stone that is easily worked) was not available in the past the builders used such stone for only the finest features. The bulk of the walls would have been of rubblestone or field flints, as in large parts

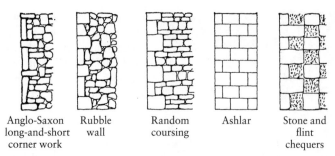

Anglo-Saxon   Rubble   Random   Ashlar   Stone and
long-and-short   wall   coursing   flint
corner work   chequers

Types of masonry.

of East Anglia. The finest stone would be brought in from other areas.

Were these rough old walls originally rendered to give them a smoother appearance and to protect the soft lime mortar between the stones from being attacked by the elements? The general view today seems to be that they were – and even painted on some occasions.

Herringbone-patterned stone masonry (so called because it resembles the bones of the fish) is a fairly good indication that the wall, or part of it, was built before the Norman invasion of 1066. Likewise what is known as 'long-and-short work' – large vertical stone slabs set alternately with horizontal slabs – in the quoins (corners) of the nave or tower usually indicates Saxon work. Brick was known to Saxon masons, but it is thought they largely reworked Roman brick.

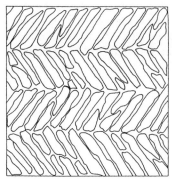

Anglo-Saxon herringboning.

There are no known brick churches in England until the re-emergence of brick-making at the end of the thirteenth century. The brick churches that date from around that time are few and far between. However, after the Reformation in the mid-sixteenth century brick began to be used again, and from about 1670 onwards it was widely used for church build-

Eighteenth-century elegance, the Church of St Mary the Virgin, Avington, Hampshire, built in brick between 1768 and 1771.

ing. In the later eighteenth and early nineteenth centuries stone replaced brick as the fashionable church-building material. Those that could not obtain it locally or afford to import it would cover their brick buildings with render, often incised with lines to imitate fine stonemasonry.

Quite often you will find churches built of different materials. While this was in all probability a matter of necessity, it can lead to some extremely attractive features. Some good examples can be found in the Welsh Marches. Here you will often find a mixture of brick or stone churches with wooden bellcotes or timber-framed towers as in the case of Upleadon, Gloucestershire. At Melverley, Shropshire, and Lower Peover, Marton and Siddington, all three in Cheshire, the entire church is timber-framed.

In areas where good building stone was sparse and the stone had to be transported great distances it has often been used to great effect. This can be seen widely all over East Anglia, in the technique known as *flushwork*, the use of finely worked freestone in combination with knapped flint to create decorative patterns flush with the wall surface.

Orientation

Is the church facing west to east? Nearly all churches face in a more or less easterly direction. However, with some modern churches because of pressure on development space it is sometimes more convenient to build the church facing other than east.

The real reason why virtually all ancient churches face east is still uncertain. It is generally accepted that the tradition stems from pagan days when the sun was seen as the source of all life and so was worshipped. Today the most commonly accepted theory is that churches face the direction in which the sun rises on the feast day of the patron saint.

One curiosity that arises from this is that you will quite often spot a chancel that is quite definitely 'off a cog' (out of true orientation) from the main body (the nave) of the church. This is usually more readily visible from the inside than the outside. It is easy to attribute this to a later rebuilding of either the main section of the church or the chancel. However, some symbolists claim that this form of building was sometimes deliberate, and represents Our Lord upon the Cross, who, on the day he died, bowed towards the right in the direction of the penitent thief. Many think this theory a little far-fetched.

A far more mundane explanation of the mystery of these 'skew chancels', or 'weeping chancels' as they are often known, is that the medieval church builders simply did not worry too much about symmetry!

Dedication

This is a practice that dates back to the early fourth century. A church is usually, but not always, dedicated to a saint. For

St Jude, Peterborough, Cambridgeshire.

example it can be dedicated to a group (All Saints, The English Martyrs) or a religious concept (Holy Cross) or an event (The Assumption). It is known that in the early days of the Church there was a very elaborate form of consecration, and the feast of dedication was celebrated annually, as it still is (see the section on Consecration Crosses, pages 40–1). The Catholic view is that the church in question is under the patronage of the saint after which it is named.

Sometimes further physical descriptions of the church were added to distinguish it from other churches nearby. So we end up with some fascinating titles, such as St Mary in the Marsh, Kent, or some of the delightful-sounding names for the City churches in London like St Mary-le-Bow and St Margaret Pattens. This also happens in many other cities.

Changes of dedication

Alterations in the dedications and patronal festivals of parish churches often indicate changes in the popularity and cults of different saints. Church records rarely tell us the reasons for such changes, nor why the parishioners decided to put themselves under the care of a different saint.

In other instances dedications changed when small churches split off from their mother churches or 'minsters', while another factor leading to change is thought to have been connected with work days and holidays.

As the dedication feast of each parish was a public holiday, and celebrated in style, parishioners were keen to make sure they did not clash with other greater festivals that brought public holidays with them. Therefore, the theory goes, they would change the

No change of dedication here: the carving of St George on his charger, slaying the dragon, still stands over the doorway of the ancient parish church at Damerham, Hampshire.

dedication of the church to spread out their holidays or 'holy-days'.

Church explorers can sometimes see the patron saint of the church they are visiting in a niche over the main south or west door.

How old is it?

Every church explorer likes to know how old a church is. The usual answer is that it has developed in several stages, and while we can roughly date the later stages it is usually a question of surmise as to the date of the original foundation. Here are some pointers:

- Take a look at the tower, if there is one. You may spot what looks like a Saxon window. Windows are an excellent guide (pages 23–6) on telling the age of a church, or sections of a church.
- Do you see any blocked windows or blocked and inserted openings in the main body of the building that can tell you anything about changes in the church's structure?

Parish churches often evolved in intriguing – and often mysterious – ways. Mixtures of materials and blocked doors and windows are sure signs of great antiquity.

- You may see the clear mark of a previous steeper-pitched roof than the present one. This is often a sign that in the last period of Gothic church architecture known as the Perpendicular (late fourteenth century to mid-sixteenth century) the roof pitch was lowered, often to accommodate more windows in the form of a clerestorey, or clearstorey. It is equally often an indication of a change of roofing material. Thatch – often the original roofing material – needs a very steep pitch for the water to run off. Often it was replaced by lead, which needs a far shallower pitch. Lead will also 'creep' off a roof if the pitch is too shallow.
- Changes of materials can perform the same function, particularly for example if the church is mainly of stone but has a brick tower or east end.
- Telling the difference between brick and stone is simple, but most joins are much harder to spot. Most churches have been added to over the years. You can often spot the joins – but what do you make of them?
- Is the outside of the church 'rough' or 'smooth'? If it is rough and gnarled and seems to be made from many different materials then it was probably originally rendered with sand and lime on the outside. Some stone churches are thought to have originally been rendered. The theory goes that the builders felt the stone was too roughly finished to be a worthy offering to God for the exterior of his house. Remember that until the nineteenth century brought mass production and cheaper transport, churches, like houses, were generally built of easily available material. If the stone is 'smooth' the church may have been built, or refaced, in the nineteenth century. If you see regular tooling and there is a rather mechanical feel to the stone then the blocks are probably nineteenth century.

It is often a good idea to return to the church (if you are able) if it is regularly floodlit. Floodlights often pick out features that are not readily discernible in daylight.

Up the wall?

While you are focusing your eyes (and binoculars if you have some) on the higher parts of the building, also take a good look at the gargoyles and waterspouts.

Gargoyles are often confused with grotesques, but there is a

Two gargoyles – carved water spouts – with grotesque carvings on their outer 'faces', where the water emerges.

difference. The word grotesque refers to any comically distorted carving in stone or timber in a church. Gargoyles are stone water-spouts, decorated with grotesque carvings. They were (and are) designed to throw the water falling on the roof or parapet away from the walls of the building. They fascinate people because of their often amusing (and frequently rude!) carvings. They can also have rather fearsome faces, but they can also be beautiful and fantastic. One theory is that because they were high up and could not be seen from ground level the masons let rip with their inventiveness: in other words they felt beyond censure. However, this theory falls down because many grotesque carvings at lower levels, particularly corbels, both inside and outside the church, are readily visible.

Another theory is that the carvers tried their best even at this level because although they knew their grotesque carvings could not be seen by men below they could be seen by God. And they wanted to give only of their best to God.

Whatever – if any – theory you choose to adhere to, keep a pair of binoculars in the car if you wish to take a good look at gargoyles on ancient parish churches.

Windows

Windows are one of the best ways of dating an ancient church from the outside and for working out which bits were added and when. All this is thanks to an architect called Thomas Rickman (1776–1841), who classified the different periods of Gothic architecture in a way that made it easy to tell the difference between the Early English, Decorated and Perpendicular styles.

Just putting the Gothic aside for a minute, you may be lucky enough to spot a pre-Conquest window (really they were more like wall openings because, in the absence of glass, we believe they were kept closed by means of shutters).

Saxon round windows

Saxon round windows were small apertures, usually formed by using wicker basketwork to keep the render in. The marks from this basketwork are the telltale feature. These windows had a deep splay (angled sill) on each side to let the light in, and therefore a very thin frame in the middle.

You will find them mainly high up in the north and south walls of some ancient East Anglian churches, where the building has survived later alterations. They were situated in that position so rain could not get in because they were protected by the overhang of the roof above the eaves. The Saxons also went in for other kinds of windows. Sometimes they had triangular heads, which you can occasionally spot in towers that date from the Saxon period. In other instances they had very narrow small, tall windows with curved heads, and again a deep splay on the inside.

Spot the Saxon window: it's the round one, characterized by a deep splay.

Norman windows

Once William the Conqueror and his Norman barons had established themselves in England they soon stamped their own form of church architecture on the land. It is described as – not un-

A typical unadorned Norman/Romanesque window.

naturally – Norman. More correctly it is known as Romanesque, because of the Norman liking for semi-circular heads over their doors and windows, a style derived from ancient Rome.

At first the Norman windows were not dissimilar from the later Saxon ones – small and with semi-circular heads. They usually set their windows high up in the wall. In Norman chancels the original small east window has often been replaced with something later and larger, but quite often the smaller round-headed side windows have been left undisturbed.

Lancet windows

Towards the end of the twelfth century church builders began to realize that arches could be pointed as well as semicircular and still be just as strong. By using pointed arches they were able to build walls that were thinner and taller. Windows that followed the same pattern allowed in much more light. These windows are known as *lancets* because of their spear or lance-like shape. They sometimes occur in threes, fives or sevens to make virtually one window, often framed by a single pointed arch.

Windows like this are easily discernible as being of the *Early English* period (late twelfth century to late thirteenth century). You will be assisted in recognizing them by the external buttresses that began to appear on the outside walls. By using these devices

Lancet window with five lights. This kind of window with a group of lancets is typical of the late Early English period, 1200–1300.

Early English lancet windows, St Mary, Uffington, Oxfordshire.

to support a building from the outside the walls could be made thinner and more space could be used for the windows.

*   *   *

Other ways of identifying churches of the Early English period can be found on page 76.

Intersecting or Y-tracery, late 13th to early 14th centuries

Geometrical tracery, early to mid-14th century

Reticulated tracery, 14th century

Decorated – the introduction of tracery.

The period of Gothic architecture generally referred to as the *Decorated* is reckoned to have started in about 1280, and this is the period in which we get involved with window *tracery*. Again you can read about this on pages 76–9. All you really need to know is that you can often tell the date of the window by its style of tracery – the interlaced pattern of ornamental stonework at the head of the window. However, that will only give you a guide to the date of the part of the building in which the window is located – not the whole building! Needless to say there was some window tracery to be found in the earlier Early English period. This is generally known as *intersecting tracery* or *Y-tracery*.

Once you have become an expert in the different styles of tracery you should always remember that windows were often replaced, openings enlarged, and new ones inserted into earlier masonry. Things are never easy with old parish churches!

A fine mid-14th-century Decorated window.

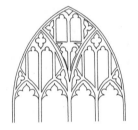

Early Perpendicular tracery.

Rectilinear or panel tracery, early to mid-16th century.

The *Perpendicular* period (*c*.1350–1550) is often described as the great flowering of English Gothic church architecture, but in fact the window patterns became simpler. The aim seems to have been (like in many buildings of today) to create 'walls of glass'. The tracery of this period was, not surprisingly, vertical and delicate. Windows of this period are wider and the arches flatter. You can read more about tracery on pages 156–7.

Windows in post-Reformation churches

As Classicism set in and the seventeenth century approached, windows became square or round-headed and had rectangular panes secured within a framework of glazing bars. Large oval windows with radiating glazing bars are also characteristic of churches of this period and will help you to recognize them from

A Venetian window of the Classical style, which came to fruition in the 18th century.

Classical windows, St Mary Woolnoth, City of London, by Hawksmoor, built 1716–27.

the outside. In the eighteenth century windows became taller, often extending to almost the full height of the building. In churches of the eighteenth century you might also spot Venetian windows from the outside. These are in three sections, with a central arched section between two lower flat-topped flanking lights.

Corbels

Corbels are brackets, usually short blocks of stone or timber that project from a wall in order to support a beam, an arch or any horizontal feature.

Exterior corbels also support the eaves of the roof at the point where they are joined by the rafters and are connected to form *corbel tables*. Many churches also have wonderful external corbel tables, which usually date from the Norman, or Romanesque, period (1066–1200). The finest ones contain a series of elaborately (and often grotesquely) carved stones. The most famous example is at the small Norman church of St Mary and St David

Corbel table above a Norman window, St Peter, Cassington, Oxfordshire.

Finely featured corbel head used as a 'spring' for an Early English chancel arch, St James, West Hanney, Oxfordshire.

at Kilpeck, Herefordshire, where there are some 80 carved corbels encircling the outside. Other fascinating examples can be seen at Elkstone in Gloucestershire, Berkswell in West Midlands, Worth Matravers in Dorset and Barfrestone in Kent.

Sundials

Sundials are another thing to look up for. There are very few Saxon ones remaining, but a notable exception is above the south doorway at St Gregory's Minster at Kirkdale in North Yorkshire, which dates from 1055.

Later church sundials are generally positioned on the church wall or porch, above the south entrance, or on a pillar in the churchyard.

People often forget that although sundials naturally helped tell both priest and congregation the time of Mass they also served the more mundane purpose of telling the time for both workers in the surrounding fields, locals and travellers. The traveller, anxious to reach his destination by nightfall, would have appreciated the ancient dial at Edstone in north Yorkshire. It bears the inscription *Orlogi Viatorum* – 'hour teller of wayfarers'.

Scratch dials and Mass dials

Scratch marks around ancient stone church doorways, and sometimes in other places, often indicate the presence of *scratch dials,* or *Mass dials*. These obscure ancient forms of sundial are often found round the south door, or on adjoining buttresses, or around the priest's door on the south-east side. In medieval churches this was designed as the priest's private entrance. In pre-Reformation times the parishioners rarely entered the chancel, which was the preserve of the priests. Nowadays priests' doors are rarely used, and they are kept locked in most old churches. But they are rich hunting grounds for Mass dials. When the church had several chantry chapels – places in which an endowment paid for a priest to say Masses for the souls of dead local grandees – the church might well have had several priests constantly saying Masses there, and perhaps even living in a room over the porch or in a small house in the grounds.

The priests had to have a way of knowing what time it was, so that they could celebrate the many Masses punctually.

Saxon scratch dial.

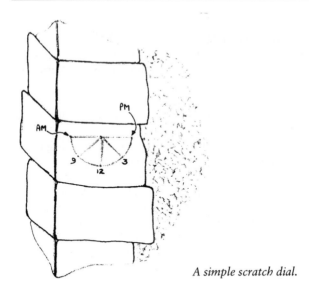

A simple scratch dial.

Mass dials are usually circular or semi-circular, and rather crudely inscribed (although some appear to have originally been very accurately cut), and often all but impossible to see by the untrained eye. However, they are one of the most fascinating and enigmatic aspects of the exterior of ancient stone churches at ground level.

In many examples of scratch or Mass dials the line which would have been reached by the shadow of the gnomon (the stick that would have been inserted to cast the sun's shadow) at 9.00 am is more clearly incised or in some way made distinct from the other lines. This is the 'Mass line' which marked the hour when the daily Mass was said on Sundays and feast days.

Some experts believe that some of these dials were so precisely carved and positioned that the sun would catch precise markings on their surface on a certain day of the year – usually that of a pre-determined saint. Another mystery surrounding these almost invisible scratchings is that distribution is amazingly uneven, and they are generally nothing like as common in the north of England as in the south. They are also hard to find in Wales.

Remains of a Mass dial, surrounded by other graffiti, including an ancient votive cross, St Mary, Uffington, Oxfordshire.

Saxon sundials are to be found at:

Cumbria: Bewcastle
Gloucestershire: Daglingworth, Saintbury
Hampshire: Corhampton, Warnford, Winchester (St Michael)
Oxfordshire: Marsh Baldon, North Stoke
Yorkshire: Great Edstone, Kirkdale, Old Byland

Other fine sundials dating from different periods are to be found outside the churches at:

Berkshire: East Garston, Farnborough
Buckinghamshire: Whaddon, Whitchurch
Carmarthenshire: Carmarthen
Cambridgeshire: Chatteris, Elton, Hemingford Grey, Wisbech
Cheshire: Disley, Runcorn (Norton Priory)
Cornwall: Lelant, Liskeard, St Columb Minor, St Wenn
Cumbria: Workington, Wreay

Derbyshire: Chapel-en-le-Frith, Eckington, Eyam, Mackworth

Devon: Buckland, Colebrooke, Filleigh, Malborough, Payhembury, Shute, Stoke Gabriel, Stowford, Tawstock Westleigh, Totnes, Winkleigh

Dorset: Belchalwell, Holnest, Piddlehinton, Silton, Sutton Waldron, Toller Porcorum

Durham: Darlington, Lanchester, Spennymoor, Staindrop, Whitburn

Essex: Boreham, Felsted, Leigh-on-Sea, Terling, Waltham Abbey

Gloucestershire: Dymock, Farmington, Great Witcombe, Hempstead, Mickleton, Naunton, Oddington, Shurdington, Tetbury,Yanworth

Gwynedd: Llandygwynnin, Penmorfa

Herefordshire: Ballingham, Donnington, Goodrich, Llangarron, Stretton Grandison, Weobley

Hertfordshire: Braughing

Kent: Chilham, Eastry, Harrietsham, Igtham, Maidstone (All Saints), Otford, Tunbridge Wells (King Charles the Martyr)

Lancashire: Chorley, Edenfield, Goosnargh, Leyland

Leicestershire: Market Harborough

Lincolnshire: Bourne, Market Deeping, Sedgebrook

London (Central): Chelsea Old Church, St Dunstan's-in-the-East, St Margaret's Westminster

London (Greater London): Isleworth, Putney

Norfolk: Hethel, Norwich (St Peter Mancroft), Wereham, Yaxham

Northamptonshire: Abington, Cold Ashby, Northampton-St Giles, Rushton, Stanwick, Stoke Albany, Weston Favell

Northumberland: Mitford, Ponteland

Oxfordshire: Cottisford, Little Faringdon, Long Wittenham, Thame

Powys: Norton

Rutland: Caldecott

Shropshire: Stokesay

Somerset: Cossington, Evercreech, North Wootton, Wedmore

Staffordshire: Alrewas, Leek

Suffolk: Ashby, Blundeston, Hadleigh, Ringsfield, Saxmundham

Sussex: Bishopstone, Catsfield, Litlington, South Malling, Southbourne

Warwickshire: Ettington, Lapworth

Wiltshire: Oaksey, Steeple Langford, Sutton Mandeville, Upper Minety

Worcestershire: Cropthorne, Elmley Castle, Grimley, Inkberrow, Netherton, Ripple

Yorkshire: Bingley, Burnby, Knaresborough, Leeds (St John), Skirlaugh, Stokesley, Tickhill,

Mass dials are also plentiful, but you will have to search carefully!
Here are some examples

Berkshire: Bucklebury

Buckinghamshire: Little Missenden, Stewkley

Cambridgeshire: Bartlow, Beetham, Girton, Hemingford Abbots, Long Stanton, Yelling

Cheshire: Audlem, Grappenhall, Great Sankey, Mobberley

Cumbria: Bolton, Dearham, Isel, Milburn

Derbyshire: Kedleston, Mackworth

Devon: Branscombe, Sidbury, Thornbury

Dorset: Portisham, Thornford

Durham: Chester-le-Street, Escomb, Hart, Pittington, Staindrop

Essex: Burnham-on-Crouch, Chipping Ongar, Elmstead, Great Leighs, Southminster, Stansted Mountfitchet

Gloucestershire: Ampney Crucis, Ampney St Mary, Berkeley, Bishop's Cleeve, Chipping Campden, Daglingworth, Eastleach Martin, Eastleach Turville, Naunton, Oldbury-on-Severn, Windrush, Yanworth

Hampshire: Ashe, Baughurst, Breamore, Hanningford, North Hayling, Romsey Abbey, Warnford

Herefordshire: Ledbury

Hertfordshire: Great Amwell, Ridge

Huntingdon district: Godmanchester

Kent: Barfrestone, Kenardington, Patrixbourne, Selling, Woodchurch

Leicester: Appleby Magna, Grendon, Houghton-on-the Hill

Lincolnshire: Fulbeck, Leadenham, Old Somerby, Winthorpe

Norfolk: Acle, Catfield, Bunwell, Chedgrave, Hales, Happisburgh, Ketteringham, Little Melton, Moulton, Redenhall, Shropham, Tittleshall, Worthing

Northamptonshire: Cogenhoe, Farthinghoe, Grafton Regis,
  Moreton Pinkney, Pottespury
Northumberland: Bywell St Peter
Nottinghamshire: Bunny, South Scarle
Oxfordshire: Brize Norton, Fulbroook, Fyfield, Hanwell, Horley,
  Hornton, Lyford, Standlake, Stanton Harcourt, Uffington, West
  Challow, West Hanney, Woolstone
Rutland: Tixover
Shropshire: Clee St Margaret, Shifnal
Somerset: Charlinch, East Brent, Martock
Staffordshire: Alrewas, Church Eaton, Croxall, Kings Bromley
Suffolk: Blythburgh, Brandeston, Bungay, Cavendish,
  Dennington, Earl Soham, Grundisburgh, Lavenham, Spexhall,
  Sternfield, Ufford
Surrey: Compton, Ockham, Stoke D'Abernon
Sussex: Alfriston, Bishopstone, East Dean, West Thorney
Warwickshire: Chadshunt, Clifford Chambers, Norton Lindsey,
  Packwood, Whichford, Wixford
Wiltshire: Ashton Keynes, Boyton, Inglesham, Salisbury-St Martin,
  Stockton
Worcestershire: Alvechurch, Astley, Bredon, Cleeve Prior,
  Himbleton, Overbury, Pirton, Stoulton
Yorkshire: Aldborough, Bilton, Driffield, Ganton, Harewood old
  church, Kirkby Malzeard, Londesborough, Newton Kyme

Other exterior markings

The sharp-eyed church explorer will find all sorts of weird markings incised in the stone at ground level or very little higher. These
can vary from masons' marks to graffiti and votive crosses. Votive
crosses are primitive small crosses scratched in stonework or on a
church door to commemorate the making of a vow. They might
have been made by travellers – or even by knights or crusaders. At
the ancient church of St John Baptist, Berkswell, Warwickshire,
some small grotesque masks carved under the eaves are said to
have been carved to protect the church from the influence of evil.

Masons' marks tend to be basic geometrical shapes, stylized
initials, lines and angles with an additional stroke or figure to

make them individual. Some you spot might have the outline of birds or animals. The mark identified the mason's personal work and his output. Some experts are able to use them as a guide to the exact date when parts of a church were built and also, when the church is all of the same period, or how long it took to build it. For the church explorer, trying to interpret these marks can be a minefield. However, it can also be great fun and you can really go to town on this aspect of church exploring!

You may, perhaps with the aid of the church guide book, occasionally be able to spot a gem of an odd carving. In the porch at St Mary's church, Elmley Castle in Worcestershire, there are some eleventh- and twelfth-century carvings of animals, including one clearly identifiable as a rabbit.

Even stranger is the odd mythical figure with the head of a man and the hindquarters and tail of a lion scratched into a stone low in the wall by the main door in the small parish church at North Cerney, Gloucestershire. Nobody really knows why it is there. One theory is that it was copied from a book of illustrations used by the creators of brass memorials. There must be many other weird markings of this sort visible to those who have a trained eye.

Rare Saxon external carving of the Virgin and Child, Deerhurst Priory Church, Gloucestershire.

Other deeply incised marks in the external stone of churches, often in and around porches, have sometimes been ascribed to arrow sharpening. This is quite a plausible theory because (see Part 4, The Churchyard) the churchyard was often used for target practice for village archers. At the same time, there may be strange markings near the porch, like the one at Awliscombe, near Honiton, Devon, which depicts a woman's hand, known locally as the 'bride's hand', and is probably associated with an old fertility rite.

Anchorites' cells

Anchorites were religious recluses living solitary lives of silence, prayer and mortification. Often they were women. They believed in a life of withdrawal and lived in tiny cells, often built into the outer walls of the chancel, where their food and sustenance was brought to them. Some lived by means of an endowment; wealthy patrons would sometimes maintain anchorites to say Masses for their ancestors. Sometimes an odd arrangement of stones low down on the outside wall of a church, often on the north side of the sanctuary, might indicate the former presence of an anchorite's cell. It is thought that anchorites' cells were also sometimes constructed inside churches, perhaps as watching places above shrines. At the church of St Mary in Kidwelly, West Wales, it is thought that such an arrangement existed, while at St Nicholas's church at Compton in Surrey it is thought that it took the form of an elevated chapel supported by the main roof pillars.

Anchorite's cell on north wall of the church, Chipping Ongar, Essex.

Anchorite's cell, Lindsell, Essex.

From early records experts are led to believe that the main period during which the practice of placing anchorites in cells took place was from about 1225 to 1400. There must be the remains of hundreds of anchorites' cells to be spotted by those who know what to look for, and where.

Other churches where it is believed that there were anchorites' cells:

Cornwall: Tintagel
Durham: Chester-le-Street
Essex: Chipping Ongar, Lindsell
Kent: Hartlip
Newcastle upon Tyne: (St John Baptist)
Norfolk: Norwich (St Julian), Trunch, King's Lynn (All Saints)
Surrey: Bletchingley, Shere
Sussex: Hardham
Yorkshire: Skipton

Exterior roods

Roods (the word comes from the Old English word *rod*, meaning cross) are carved images of Christ crucified. The ancient Saxon ones are invariably of stone and usually set in the outer walls of ancient churches – usually near the door. Being Saxon, they are rare, but it is possible to view them at the churches at Bitton and Wormington, both in south Gloucestershire; at Daglingworth, near Cirencester in Gloucestershire; at Langford in Oxfordshire; and at Breamore, Headbourne Worthy and Romsey, which are all in Hampshire.

Consecration crosses

Many church explorers are familiar with these inside a church because they were sometimes incised as well as painted on church walls. Originally there were 12 of them and they were often painted quite high up, so that they would not be brushed and obliterated by the clothes of passers-by. They are not to be confused with Stations of the Cross, also to be found inside many churches.

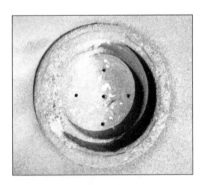

Exterior consecration cross, Church of St Mary, Uffington, Oxfordshire.

The exterior consecration crosses, also 12 in number, were sometimes simply just anointed onto the walls using oil, so there is often no remaining evidence. However, where external consecration crosses were incised into the stone or painted on (usually in red within a circle) they can occasionally still be found. They are rare, but good examples of exterior crosses can be seen at

Remains of a consecration cross above the blocked north door, Little Faringdon, Oxfordshire.

Uffington, Oxfordshire; at Ottery St Mary, Devon; at Edington, Wiltshire; and at Moorlinch, Somerset.

Look down!

You can read about various kinds of gravestone in Part 4, but in some instances it is possible to see clear evidence of an earlier church because the present building has been built within the ruined walls of the previous church or using just a part of the previous church. There are some good examples of this in East Anglia.

At Walberswick in Suffolk the large fifteenth-century church was robbed of its tithes under Henry VIII and later in the sixteenth century much of its interior was despoiled by Protestant elements. At the time of the Restoration – 1660 – the church-wardens were required to put the building into good repair, but little was done and the church fell into a very dilapidated state. Almost 100 years later the decision was taken to remove the roof of the nave chancel and north aisle and sell the materials, turning the south aisle into the parish church that we see today, set among the ruins of the original building.

St Andrew, Covehithe, Suffolk: the present small thatched church, built into the walls of the old, dates from 1672. It was built after the great 15th-century church became very run down and the decreasing population was no longer able to afford to maintain it.

At Covehithe, also in Suffolk, the original tower and the external walls of the huge fourteenth- and fifteenth-century church remains, but most of the present tiny thatched church built within the ruins dates from 1672. It is generally believed that the reason for the contraction was that a shrinking population at the time was unable to maintain such a large church.

Another good example is at Oxborough, in Norfolk. Here, looking around this peaceful scene from a distance you would scarcely imagine that a tower collapse as recent as 1948 demolished the nave and most of the south side of the fifteenth-century church and that the present church is the original chancel and south chapel, complete with its magnificent terracotta tombs.

After the collapse it was decided that the chancel would provide a church big enough to serve the village, and the nave was left roofless. For the church explorer it is rather hard to work out – unless he or she has read about it before.

Thatched churches

It seems quite likely that all ancient churches had thatched roofs, if they date back far enough. Norfolk has 57 thatched churches, mainly in the area surrounding the Broads, traditionally a water-reed growing area. Suffolk has thatched churches at Ashby, Barsham, Covehithe, Icklingham (All Saints), Ixworth, Rush-mere, Theberton, Thornham Parva, Thorpe (St Michael) and Westleton.

St Margaret, Hales: one of 57 thatched churches in Norfolk. It dates from around 1150. There are also several dozen thatched churches in Suffolk, some of them dating from Saxon times.
(Photo: 'Lyn Stilgoe)

Some Norfolk thatched churches to explore

Many of the loveliest (and oldest) are also round-towered (see pages 63–5) Of these a number are believed to date from Saxon times. They include:

Fritton: formerly near the coast, but now a few miles inland.
Hales: (see photo on previous page): regarded by many as the archetypal old thatched church on account of its rugged walls and interesting east end, which has sturdy Norman arcading round the outside.
Heckingham: this church is near to Hales and resembles it in several ways. Like Hales it is extremely rural, and administered by the Churches Conservation Trust.
Potter Heigham: this has a tower regarded as Saxon. The nave and chancel date from the fifteenth century.
Mautby: the long thatched roof stretches unbroken over both nave and chancel.
Stockton: this church has a miniature lead-covered spire surmounting its ancient round tower
Thorpe next Haddiscoe: this church has much attractive flintwork

Suffolk

Suffolk also has a number of thatched churches, many of them with Saxon origins. Some of the loveliest are at: Ashby, Barsham, Bramfield, Covehithe, Herringfleet, Icklingham (All Saints), Ixworth Thorpe, Rushmere St Michael, Theberton, Thornham Parva and Westleton. Again, many of these have round towers.

Other thatched churches are rare, but you will find them in the following counties:

Essex: Silver End
Herefordshire: Brockhampton (All Saints)
Isle of Wight: Freshwater Bay, St Agnes
Lincolnshire: Markby

2

External Features

*I'm afraid he has not been in the inside of a church for many
years; but he never passes a church without pulling off his hat.
This shows that he has good principles.*
Samuel Johnson

Doors

If you walk round the church, note the doorways. The main door
to the church will normally be to the south. This was the side of
the churchyard more regularly frequented than the north side,
which was widely believed by many to be haunted and the home
of evil spirits (see Part 4, The Churchyard).

The north door was usually kept firmly closed, but it was
opened during baptism services to allow the evil spirits to escape.
It was also used, as well as the great west door – if there was one

*Example of a fine late
Perpendicular south
doorway at Layer Marney,
Essex.*

– for outdoor processions. However, when processions were discouraged after the Reformation north doors were often blocked. Today the blocked north door is a common sight, to be seen in old churches all over the country. It is often one of the first things to be spotted on your initial walk round the church.

Today in most parish churches the north door, unless for some reason it is used as the main entrance, is kept permanently closed. This is often for the very practical purpose of preventing draughts.

In medieval times doorways were, as a rule, the most decorative features of small parish churches and practically every parish church has a north and south door, usually towards the west end of the nave. It is obviously the old churches that have the most fascinating doors because they often tell stories. The door of St Botolph's church at Hadstock, Essex, has been dated to around 1020 and is thought to be the oldest church door in the country.

Tradition has it that a Dane was punished for committing sacrilege by being flayed alive and his skin nailed to the door. When the door was repaired a piece of human skin was found under one of the hinges and is now in the nearby Saffron Walden Museum.

The door stands to this day, strengthened by three great wrought-iron strap hinges, doubtless created by a local blacksmith.

It all goes to show that, just as the church explorer has much to learn from pacing round the building carefully before entering, so the door, as well as the porch, can often tell a story.

Sanctuary rings

Some ancient doors still have ancient *sanctuary rings* or their bosses attached to them. These were quite common in the past when the right of sanctuary existed in all parish churches and cathedrals. The church would offer sanctuary to any fugitive, whether from justice or from fear of his enemies, until a trial could be arranged.

The period of sanctuary was usually 40 days, during which time the fugitive was perfectly safe in the church and officers of the law could only seek by argument to induce him to go into

Sanctuary ring, Dormington, Hereford and Worcester.

Sanctuary ring, Durham Cathedral.

banishment. If he agreed to banishment he was dressed in a white robe or sackcloth and carrying a wooden cross would travel to an agreed port and board the first available ship.

The right of sanctuary was abolished in the seventeenth century.

Fine examples of sanctuary rings or knockers can be found at:

Devon: Talaton
Essex: Fingringhoe
Herefordshire: Dormington
Norfolk: Norwich (St Gregory)
Oxfordshire: Westcott Barton
Powys: Rhulen
Shropshire: Cound
Suffolk: Brightwell, Burgh, Dennington, Great Bealings, Ufford
Yorkshire: Adel, York (All Saints)

Styles of doorway

Saxon

Early Saxon doorways are usually high and narrow, with the door head being either gable-ended composed of two stones forming two sides of a triangle, or semicircular, with the lintel formed of shaped stones. To relieve and discharge the weight of the lintel, an arch was often built above the lintel. This space is called the tympanum, and in Norman times it very often received decorative treatment.

Saxon doorway, Stow-in-Lindsey, Lincolnshire. On the left is long-and-short stonework.

Norman

In the Norman, or Romanesque, period doorways continued to be semicircular, but became true arches constructed of separate wedge-shaped stones called *voussoirs*. Doors of this period (1066–1200) often have richly decorated tympana, often depicting biblical stories or insignia. Quite often the carving is exhuberant and forms one of the main items of appeal in the church. In an English Norman (Romanesque) church the tympanum is quite often the main point of interest.

Richly ornamented Norman doorway, St Mary and St David, Kilpeck, Herefordshire.

Study in development: finely wrought late Perpendicular window above Norman doorway, St Mary, Bampton, Oxfordshire.

Early English

During the transitional period between the Norman and Early English periods, arches, including those above doorways, gradually became slightly pointed as the Gothic style began to make its mark. Some of the best Early English doorways have several orders of shafts on each side. Dog tooth ornamentation is a feature of the period. This is a form of repetitive decoration round doorways and arches. It takes its name from the large rear teeth of dogs, because

Early English door.

the ornamentation comes in groups of two or four tooth-like projections in a hollow moulding. As in Norman times the doors of this period were generally covered with ironwork

Decorated (1300–50)

As its name indicates, this form of the Gothic is recognized by its decoration. In doorways of churches of this period look out for ballflower decoration. Typical examples resemble small balls half enclosed by a globular flower, which has three petals that curve in. With doorways of this period you are also likely to find fewer shafts, or pillars, on each side. The moulding round the door will probably therefore be continuous. These mouldings are likely to be deeper cut than Early English doorways, and the arches slightly more depressed.

Perpendicular (1350-1550)

The pointed arches of both doorways and windows became more depressed during this period. The most characteristic feature was the framing of the arch in a rectangular hood-mould, usually with a spandrel (the triangular area between the top corners of the arch) and the hood-mould in each corner. These spandrels are often richly carved, usually with the coats of arms of local great families who endowed the church, or with sacred emblems. Some have Tudor roses or foliage.

Some of the larger Perpendicular doors have smaller wicket doors within them. Examples are at Gedney, Lincolnshire, and at Thaxted, Essex.

Just a few of the many other fine old doors are to be found at:

Devon: Dartmouth (St Saviour)
Essex: Buttsbury, Eastwood Great Bardfield, Hadstock, Shalford
Herefordshire: Abbey Dore, Dormington, Monnington on Wye, Pembridge
Hertfordshire: Little Hormead
Lincolnshire: Addlethorpe
Norfolk: Harpley, Salle
Oxfordshire: Faringdon, North Stoke
Somerset: Wellow
Suffolk: Blythburgh, Dennington, Great Bealings, St Mary-at-the-Elms, Ipswich, Stoke-by-Nayland, Stonham Parva
Surrey: Send
Yorkshire: Adel, Skipwith

Norman door carving/tympana

These are quite fascinating in many of the famous Norman churches in England and Wales. The Normans incorporated all manner of motifs in the sculptural decoration of their doorways, arches, capitals and tympana. You will see animal and human

*An early Norman tympanum at St Peter's
Charney Bassett, Oxfordshire. It shows a man
standing holding two gryphons, which are
biting him.*

figures, biblical scenes, serpents and monsters. Scholars are per-
plexed as to the origins of all this.

What is even more odd is that although the so-called 'Norman'
style is only the English version of a pan-European style of the
eleventh and twelfth the centuries known as Romanesque, the
beakhead ornament, in which the heads of birds and beasts were
carved in hollow mouldings so that the beaks or tongues over-
lapped into adjoining mouldings, is typically to be found in this
country.

Sometimes the doorway was considered so valuable that when
a new church was built or the church was reordered or extended
or a new porch was built, the entire doorway was moved. A good
example is the church of St Michael, at Guiting Power in
Gloucestershire.

Porches

If there is a porch of note this is a bonus – even if you can't get in
the church. Indeed, most churches have porches and there is good
reason to believe that all ancient churches had them because of
the major part the porch played in the life of the church.

*This heavily ornamented door surround is
Victorian work. It was added to the Wren church
of St Michael, Cornhill, in the City of London by
Sir George Gilbert Scott.*

So if you find yourself in the porch of an ancient church shelter-
ing from the rain, or trying to open the door or searching for the
name and number of a keyholder to phone, take a good look.

If the porch was added to the building during the Perpendicular
period (1350–1550) or replaced an earlier one then it will probably be quite grand – possibly of more than one storey. This is
because in prosperous areas in the fifteenth and sixteenth
centuries – their prosperity usually arose out of a wool-based
economy – it was common for the south aisle to be rebuilt by one
of the local guilds or a wealthy local benefactor. The porch was
often added at the same time.

Grand porches at this time would probably have had large
stone benches along each side. Porches, after all, had always been
used as resting-places for people travelling long distances to rest

Elaborate three-storey porch of the Perpendicular period, St John the Baptist, Burford, Oxfordshire.

in before services. So, as a visitor, why not avail yourself of this and sit down and inspect the rest of the porch?

Take a look at the doorway in the porch, particularly if it is elaborately carved and predates the porch itself. In this case the carving should have been well preserved. This happens a great deal on Norman churches when there was a desire to protect the fine doorway. This is one reason why we have so many well-preserved exquisitely carved Norman doorways still in good condition today.

Things to look out for in church porches

Look out for wonderful *vaulted ceilings*. You are likely to find these in churches of the late Gothic (Perpendicular) period – or added at this time to earlier churches. Vaults are the arched framework of a stone roof, and in fine stone porches they are intersected by stone *ribs* (curved stone supports) to produce a striking effect. Often stone bosses or heraldry of some sort will be incorporated.

Fine porch with Norman/Romanesque doorway and unusual wall niche in the Decorated style, St Mary, Kempsford, Gloucestershire. Note the stone benches on either side: they would have served as a resting place for funeral corteges and played a major part in 'porch weddings'.

Fine old oak Welsh border-lands porch, St Peter, Melverley, Shropshire: one of two timber-framed churches in the county.

People often fail to realize the many roles the porch used to play. The original functions of the porch were the obvious ones of providing shelter for parishioners and to protect the door from the elements. However, they were also used for the first part of the baptism and wedding services and as a resting-place for the funeral cortege before moving on to the chancel. They were also used for the service of churching of women after childbirth.

Very rarely you will find a *piscina* – a niche set in the wall in which the priest would wash his hands before the Mass – in a church porch, indicating that altars almost certainly existed in some church porches. It is believed that in front of them, or in front of the niches that accommodated saints' effigies, oaths were sworn and contracts signed. Justice was also sometimes administered in the church porch.

Piscinas – rare in church porches – are not to be confused with *holy water stoups*, which are quite common and still used in some

Two- and three-storey porches:

Bristol: St Mary Redcliffe
Dorset: Loders
Essex: Saffron Walden, Thaxted
Gloucestershire: Northleach, Painswick
Kent: Cranbrook
Norfolk: Acle, Aylmerton, Cley, Fakenham, Hempnall, Hevingham,
    Ingham, King's Lynn (St Nicholas), Loddon, Pulham St Mary,
    Redenhall, Weybourne, Worstead, Wymondham
Oxfordshire: Chipping Norton, Shipton-under-Wychwood
Shropshire: Ludlow
Suffolk: Blythburgh, Fressingfield, Mendlesham, Woolpit
Warwickshire: Lapworth
Wiltshire: Tisbury

At least six medieval churches in Norwich have two two-storey
porches.

   At Astbury in Cheshire, at Burford in Oxfordshire, at
Cirencester in Gloucestershire, and at Ingham in Norfolk there
are grand three-storey porches.

churches today when visitors are encouraged to make the sign of
the cross on their foreheads, using the water provided, before they
enter the building.

   Some larger porches have *two storeys*, with a room above. This
was used for a variety of purposes. Sometimes it served as a
priest's lodging, especially when the church was served by several
priests, some of whom were supported by endowments
(chantries) left by dead grandees for the purpose of saying Masses
for their souls.

   However, they were also sometimes used as small chapels,
schoolrooms, libraries, or stores for parish chests and records. At
Mendlesham in Suffolk the porch was used, at one stage, as the
parish armoury.

   Some of these upper rooms in porches can still be visited today.
Again, large porches with rooms above usually coincided with the
Perpendicular period of church building – from 1350 to 1550.

   We generally associate grand two-storey porches with the great wool churches of the Cotswolds, East Anglia, and parts of Devon, Somerset and Lincolnshire.

Many large churches have two porches. They were originally designed to be used for processional purposes. People often forget the many processions that took place in medieval times. For the ordinary peasant they represented a change from the drudgery and routine of everyday life. The fact that they very often signified feast days, and therefore holidays, added to their enjoyment.

Towers and spires

It could be said that the *tower* stamps the look of the exterior – rather like the head or face of a human being. Again, towers very often reflect the local styles. In Devon and Cornwall there are lofty towers, often with corner turrets. Somerset church towers are often mighty creations, while East Anglia is noted for its fine flint towers and very early round towers. In Essex and parts of Herefordshire and other Welsh border counties the timber towers are worth searching for, while Essex and most south-eastern counties have many churches sporting rather attractive rustic-

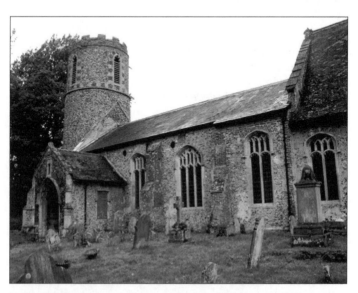

Early East Anglian round tower, St Mary, Syleham, Suffolk.

St Dunstan-in-the-East, Great Tower Street, City of London: this fine Wren lantern spire dates from the end of the 17th century. Sadly only the tower and spire of this church remain.

looking bell turrets which perch above the gable roof and usually rest upon massive timber constructions inside.

Spires are more common on churches in the Midlands. These remarkable stone constructions are actually the tower roof carried to a ridiculous extreme. The view inside the spire, looking up from belfry level, is well worth seeing if the opportunity arises.

You would be hard-pressed to find a more 'English' scene than a church with a soaring spire, especially when it caps a tower.

When the tower and spire merge into one it is called a *steeple*. Early towers had simple pitched, or sometimes pyramidal, roofs. The idea was to throw rainwater clear of the supporting walls. When a light timber-framed spire was added to an earlier tower it was often covered with lead, which gave it a grey or even white appearance. Quite often timber spires are covered with shingles – wooden tiles – because they are both light and weatherproof, and easier to fix than slates.

When a spire is entirely of stone it is a fine sight, because of the fine jointed masonry and high level of skill in forming the structure. Some of the finest examples have massive pinnacles at the corners and large dormer windows at the base on the four

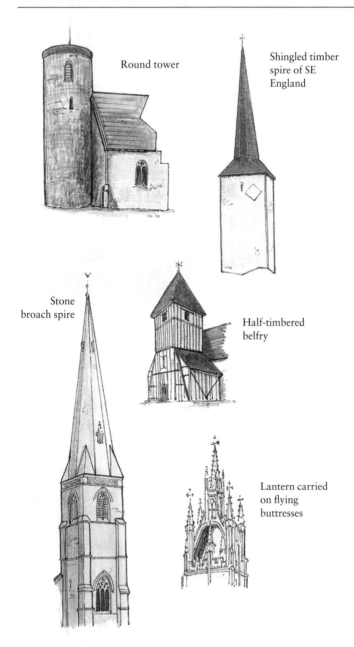

Round tower

Shingled timber spire of SE England

Stone broach spire

Half-timbered belfry

Lantern carried on flying buttresses

Detached belfry in timber:
Welsh borderlands

Fine medieval
tower and spire
with pinnacles and
flying buttresses

Perpendicular
tower

Renaissance tower
and spire

Towers and spires.

main sides. There are some excellent examples in the Oxford area. Late Gothic stone spires built in the 1400s and early 1500s are often very fine, built on top of tall towers and supported by flying buttresses. A notable feature of these late spires are the crockets – carved leaf-like decorative features in stone that project at regular intervals where the sloping sides join.

Broach spires evolved in the thirteenth century. In a broach spire the square tower changes to an octagonal spire by means of broaches, or pyramids, at the corners of the spire. Broaches vary greatly in size, from large and steep pitch to low and barely visible from the ground.

As spires developed and became ever more intricate flying buttresses, open arches (or half-arches) which 'fly' up from the parapets of the tower at the corners and help to support the spire were needed for support. This style culminated in the stone 'lantern'. This is a circular or polygonal turret-like structure with pinnacles and a short spire at the top. It is

St Mary Aldermary: one of the finest City of London churches. Sir Christopher Wren rebuilt the upper stage of the tower, which survived the Great Fire of London. It is post-medieval and the style is best described as 'Gothic survival'.

open to the elements at the centre and is supported by flying buttresses.

During the Renaissance period spires became thinner and more
sophisticated – rather like the round tiers on a wedding cake.
Modern spires tend to be very thin and are known as 'needles'.

Types of tower

Saxon (*c*.600–1066) – often small and narrow, with narrow
belfry openings divided by stone columns known as balusters.
Norman (1066–1200) – often massive, with small round-headed
openings, usually surrounded by carving.
Early English (1200–1300) – frequently much less massive than
their Norman predecessors. They have suppporting buttresses
and slender, pointed windows.
Decorated (1300–1350) – generally tall and slender, with buttresses placed at angles to the tower corners. Window openings
are large and elaborate. Towers are often decorated with niches
and pinnacles.
Perpendicular (1350–1550) – divided into several stages, with
large windows and many-tiered buttresses. They are often decorated with niches, carved panelling and pinnacles.

Round towers

There are 185 round-towered churches in England and Wales.
Of these, 127 are in Norfolk, 42 in Suffolk, 7 in Essex, 2 in
Cambridgeshire and 2 Victorian ones in Wales. The rest are in
Sussex and Berkshire.

The one thing they all have in common is that they are in flint
areas. You might think therefore that because flint is the only
building stone and it does not lend itself to large square blocks
that this was the reason for building the church towers round.

However, that does not take account of all the weird and
wonderful theories as to why these admittedly somewhat mysterious towers are attached to churches in all sorts of out-of-the-way
places. One is that they were originally wells and that when the
land subsided they were left standing, so resourceful Christians
built the rest of their churches against them!

St Mary, Haddiscoe, Norfolk.   *St Andrew, Little Snoring, Norfolk.*

Another theory links the round towers and the great stone rings of prehistory like Stonehenge. This theory says that the round towers were the original sites of worship, with the conventional rectangular buildings added later. Round churchyards have quite often been linked with ancient pagan sites, but it is difficult to see how a round *tower* fitted into all this.

A slightly more credible theory is that some or many of the towers were originally built for defence against Viking raids, or as lookout posts. However, the Viking raids were almost over before the first-known date of any round-tower church. Many experts, however, hold to the theory the towers were originally both look-out towers and belltowers, in remote areas where the building stone was poor. Many of them date from before the Norman Conquest – days when bells played a far more significant part in attracting the attention of the neighbourhood than they do today.

Although a handful of round-towered churches were built in Victorian times the majority of round towers occur in areas where good building stone was scarce. They therefore – like the churches they are usually attached to – are fascinating to look at because of

Welsh borderlands church with detached belfry, St Leonard, Yarpole, Herefordshire.

their often rugged and homespun appearance. Their walls are characterized by the variety of rough rubblestones, field flints and (near the sea) boulders from the beach. In remote areas of Norfolk where they sometimes represent the only building in a former hamlet, some round towers also have lumps of local ferricrete – a naturally occuring conglomerate found on the surface of the fields – in the walls, as well as lumps of carstone, a local sandstone that occurs in small deposits, and sometimes reused Roman tiles.

The Round Tower Churches Society (<u>www.roundtowers.org.</u> <u>uk</u>) was established in 1973. Its aims are to generate interest in these fascinating churches and to raise money to give repair and restoration grants.

Detached towers and belfries

Nearly 40 churches in England and Wales have detached towers and belfries. There are all sorts of reasons given for this, from defence, as in the case of Westbury-on-Severn, Gloucestershire, to weight, as in the case of Brookland, Kent, where the unusual bell tower was built as a detached structure because of the soft ground on Romney Marsh. Another famous example is East Bergholt in Suffolk, where the detached wooden bell house was built, it is thought, as a temporary structure when work on the incomplete west tower ceased, and has remained ever since.

Churches with detached towers and belfries:

Bedfordshire: Elstow, Marston Moretaine
Cambridgeshire: Tydd St Giles
Cornwall: Feock, Gunwalloe, Gwennap, Mylor
Cumbria: Kirkoswald
Gloucestershire: Westbury on Severn
Herefordshire: Bosbury, Holmer, Ledbury, Pembridge, Richards Castle, Yarpole
Kent: Brookland
Lincolnshire: Fleet
Norfolk: East Dereham, Little Snoring, Terrington St Clement, West Walton
Northamptonshire: Irthlingborough
Powys: Bronllys
Suffolk: Beccles, Bramfield, East Bergholt
Swansea: Llangyfelach

So, if sometimes the church proves impossible to enter, the enthusiastic explorer will at least have more time to explore the outside of the building. And after all, if you have seen the exterior, you have seen half the church!

PART 2

Basic Church Design and Architecture

3

A Brief History

A church and a chapitle,
Wonderfuly wel y-bild,
With niches on everiche half,
And bellyche y-corven;
With crotchetes on corneres,
With knottes of gold,
With gay glitering glas
Glowyng as the sunne . . .
Langland, *Piers Plowman*

Having wandered round the outside of the church looking for clues as to why it is there, you might find it useful to have a brief knowledge of church architecture and how it has evolved from Saxon times.

Most old churches in England and Wales have evolved in a fairly haphazard way, to suit the needs of the local population, which is a major reason why church exploring is such interesting detective work. Unravelling the fluctuating fortunes of a community through the architectural development and contents of the parish church is the key to the real pleasure to be gained from church exploring. This is the fun part. However, you will gain a lot more from your church exploring if you learn a little of the background information that will make your visits to churches much more enjoyable.

Whichever way you go about it, this will need a certain amount of mugging up. You can do this from library books or books you may already possess. Alternatively, you can read this chapter.

If you wish to get straight on with your church exploring, or are standing in the pouring rain trying to get into a church, then miss out this chapter and try to read it at a later stage.

* * *

St Peter, Wootton Wawen, Warwickshire: this church looks from the outside as though it dates largely from the 15th century and is built in Perpendicular style, but inside there is a Saxon sanctuary, dating from five hundred years earlier.

The Saxon period: 600–1066

The Romans left Britain at the beginning of the fifth century and their departure encouraged the arrival of successive invasions of Germanic settlers (Saxons) from across the North Sea. The origins of Christianity in this country are hazy. However, we know from the writings of Bede, an eighth-century Northumbrian monk, that a successful mission had been sent from Pope Gregory in Rome to Kent under Augustine in 597. We are equally hazy about the origins of the first churches, but it seems probable that Christianity developed at different rates in differing parts of the country.

Like the Romans, the Saxons went for round arches, but with them the emphasis was on height rather than breadth, possibly because the first churches might also have acted as a means of defence.

Escomb, Co. Durham: the parish church of St John is widely regarded as England's earliest complete Anglo-Saxon church.

In Saxon churches windows were small, and generally quite high off the ground. Although the Romans had used semicircular arches on a massive scale the Saxon builders were far more timid. Their churches usually have doorways and windows that are narrower and bridged at the top with a flat stone. When wider openings were needed in Saxon churches the builders would lean two stones inward on each other to make a triangular head to the door or window. Sometimes both semicircular and triangular heads can be seen in the same building.

Windows were usually *splayed*. A splay is when a window is given a sloping edge. The idea in Saxon times was to bring in more light and ventilation through what was usually an extremely thick wall. Sometimes the splays were of the *double* variety – that is, they were placed on both the inside and the outside.

Anglo-Saxon double-splayed window.

Anglo-Saxon herringbone work.

In Saxon churches the heads of doorways usually followed a similar pattern to those of windows. Normally the jambs are plain, and arches rest on horizontal stones set in the wall and called *imposts*.

On the outside Saxon masonry is very distinctive. One of its best-known features is *long-and-short work* at the corner of the building, and in particular the tower. The stones at the corners – the *quoins* – are alternately upright and horizontal. The Saxons were also very fond of patterned masonry, and two other tell-tale features of their work are *pilaster strips* and *herringboning.*

Pilaster strips are vertical strips of stone that stand out very slightly from the wall. Their use is purely decorative but is a sure sign of Anglo-Saxon work. Good examples are to be seen at Earls Barton, Northamptonshire, and at Sompting in West Sussex, Repton in Derbyshire and Barnack in Cambridgeshire. In herringbone work, stones of one course all slope to the right while the stones of the course above it slope to the left, and so on. Saxon masonry was usually covered with plaster, traces of which can sometimes be seen.

As the church explorer becomes more experienced – that is, views more and more churches – it is possible to get a feel for a church that was probably originally Saxon, even if none of these characteristically Saxon features are to be seen in it any longer. This usually arises from the proportions. If the nave – the main body of the church – appears to be excessively tall in relation to its width, then there is a chance the present walls could well be built on a Saxon plan. Similarly the chancel: if the chancel arch (if there is one) is again tall and narrow and the chancel is only slightly narrower than the nave, then this could again be a sign of a Saxon plan.

Western towers were common in Saxon churches and nearly 70 survive in England alone. You are more likely to see them in the eastern counties. Northumberland, Durham, Lincolnshire and East Anglia are particularly strong on Saxon churches – which is understandable when you consider that the successive waves of Saxon invaders first settled in the east of the country.

It was careful measuring plus a strong hunch and much inspiration that led to the rediscovery, in 1856, of the little Saxon church of St Lawrence at Bradford-on-Avon, Wiltshire. This famous seventh-century Saxon church had been divided up and put to all manner of uses, including as a schoolroom, until a keen church explorer tried out a theory with a tape measure and the church was rediscovered. Today it is one of the most visited churches in England.

Who knows what discoveries are out there waiting to be made?

Norman/Romanesque: 1066–1200

The Normans built in the style known elsewhere in Europe as Romanesque, because it was based on the Roman idea of the rounded arch.

'Energetic', 'massive' and 'distinctive' are adjectives frequently applied to Norman churches, which are characterized by their very thick walls, rather squat, square towers and massive interior columns, which were usually round or square, with bases to match.

Norman doorways are also characterized by their rounded arches, frequently ornamented by zig-zag and other ornamental carving, and sometimes surmounted by a decorated or carved stone *tympanum* – the solid space between the top of the door and the arch shape above it. Windows in churches of this period also usually have round arches. They are often heavily ornamented. As well as zig-zags, typical Norman motifs are billetts (short raised rectangles repeated at regular intervals), barrels, stars and beak-heads (see photo on page 53).

The Norman is a much-loved style because it is highly distinctive. It is also rather obvious and logical, and people like to think it tells us something about the organization and orderliness of these Norman invaders who imposed their ideas and culture so very definitely upon the native British people.

Where to find Saxon and Norman churches

Good examples of *Saxon towers* are to be seen at St Peter, Barton-upon-Humber in Lincolnshire, Wickham in Berkshire, Earls Barton in Northamptonshire, Oxford (St Michael-at-the North-gate) and Sompting in Sussex.

You will find very few complete Saxon churches in England, but many with remnants from this period. In contrast, wonderful examples of Norman churches are to be found all over England from Christchurch, Dorset, and East Meon, Hampshire, to Iffley in Oxfordshire, Stewkley in Buckinghamshire, Walsoken in Norfolk, Old Shoreham in Sussex, Castor in Northamptonshire and Sandwich in Kent.

Norman doorway, St Mary the Virgin, Iffley, Oxfordshire.

How the Gothic arrived

The three key phases to remember in conjunction with the Gothic architecture are Early English, Decorated and Perpendicular. The church explorer needs to know what the terms mean and broadly the years these periods spanned. Apart from that, when you think Gothic think *Pointed Arches.* Then you can't go far wrong.

So the Gothic style is characterized by the pointed arch: but how did this replace the curved arch?

Fine Decorated doorway (c.1300).

There are all sorts of theories here: scholars are always arguing and books are still being written about it.

What seems fact is that the medieval church builders found that with the pointed arch the *vaulting* – the arched interior framework of the roof – could afford all sorts of exciting possibilities that had not been possible with simple curved arches. Foremost among these was the formation of *arcades*, a whole series of arches supported by columns or piers, that soon formed one of the great hallmarks of early Gothic architecture.

With pointed arches it was possible to build a vault rising to a uniform height throughout, whereas with the old semicircular pattern the arches along the sides and diagonals of a rectangular structure obviously rose to three different heights and made vaulting a serious problem.

By having thinner walls and arcades of internal pillars it was possible for the builders of this period to construct churches that were taller and more elegant.

It seems sensible to assume that all this was a gradual evolution rather than an overnight change, and so churches built from around 1150 to 1200 or so are often referred to as 'transitional'.

Early English: 1200–1300

This style is also known as 'first pointed' or 'lancet'. These have already been described in Part 1, page 25.

The Early English church builders often made their buildings as austere as possible as a symbol of the renunciation of the flesh and of worldly riches. In this they were heavily influenced by the ideas and skills of the craftsmen who were sent from the continent to build fine new abbeys as outposts of the great religious houses in Burgundy.

Churches of this period usually have more elaborate towers than their Norman predecessors. They also quite often have broach spires. These are octagonal and rise from the top of a tower without a parapet (see *spires*, page 59).

The whole object seems to have been to try to avoid the massive nature of Norman/Romanesque churches, and to aim for increased internal space and height – something altogether more sophisticated and elegant. Walls were thinner, pierced in order to achieve larger areas of window. *Buttresses* – tall wall supports built against the outside walls of the building – began to appear. These had been used very little in Saxon and Norman buildings because they generally had thick walls, and little reinforcement was needed. However, with thinner walls buttresses were obviously needed more.

Internally the chunky round columns of the Norman period were replaced by compound columns of cylindrical or octagonal shafts

Decorated: 1300–50

The Early English period merged into what we generally call the *Decorated Gothic*, *Middle Pointed* or *Flamboyant* period. Further developments in buttressing led to the thinner walls and wider windows that characterize this style. The masons became far more adventurous – even reckless, according to some critics of architecture of the period – and wished to show all the amazing things they could do with stone. The result is far more exciting architecture and construction of churches than was associated with the Early English period.

The Decorated period saw the introduction, outside the church,

Fine church interior containing work from all three Gothic periods.
St Agnes, Cawston, Norfolk. (Photo: Richard Tilbrook)

*The Decorated Gothic.
Above: capitals at St Patrick,
Patrington, East Riding of
Yorkshire. Left: doorway at
St Lawrence, Keyston,
Cambridgeshire. Below: delicate
window tracery from the
Decorated period at St Mary,
Chatham, Kent.*

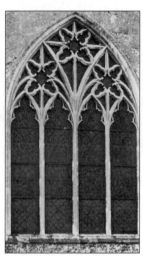

of larger and more elaborate buttresses, often set at an angle to the corners of the building. Interior vaulting became more complicated, with arrangements of *ribs* (curved stone supports) becoming more and more elaborate. More of this is explained in Part 3, Inside the Church.

Towers in the Decorated (or Late Gothic) period often have battlemented parapets, often pinnacled at the corners. You will also see the occasional fine sight of a *flying buttress* leading from the corners or pinnacles of the parapets to the spire. It is easier to identify the window tracery from the inside, but it is characterized by geometric forms (early Decorated period) and then later sinuous flowing lines in the stone tracery (see page 156).

Perpendicular: 1350–1550

This period – the latter part of the fourteenth century through to the mid-sixteenth century – was the great age of English church building, characterized by soaring upward lines in great windows and towers that are often extremely high and decorated with

Long Melford, Suffolk: late 15th-century Perpendicular.

panels and fretted stonework. In the largest and finest parish churches of this period the external buttresses are a very important feature of the architecture. In earlier churches buttresses – tall wall supports built against the outside walls of the building – were

Perpendicular door

important to counteract the vast weight of roofs and towers and to compensate for the structurally weakening effects of window openings. By the Perpendicular period the very high stone vaults, slender walls and vast windows with grid-like tracery demanded elaborate and often very tall buttresses, sometimes at roof height, with pinnacles to add extra weight to counteract the outward thrust of all this masonry.

The Perpendicular is a peculiarly English style – something many church explorers do not realize – and very much the expression of an extremely affluent period in the nation's fortunes. It can be seen at its best in areas made wealthy by the wool trade such as Gloucestershire (the Cotswolds), East Anglia and Somerset.

After this we reach the end of the Gothic.

The Reformation

As every school student is taught, this was the great religious revolution of the sixteenth century, when a number of European states broke away from the Roman Catholic Church and the authority of the Pope and adopted some form of Protestant belief. In England the Reformation was pretty cataclysmic for both Church and State. It resulted in Henry VIII's break with Rome and rejection of papal authority following the dissolution of his marriage with Catherine of Aragon. The date to remember is 1534. In this year a series of Acts of Parliament severed financial, judicial and administrative links with Rome and eventually, in 1539, led to the first authoritative statement (the Six Articles) of the doctrines of the English Church. As a result of the new Acts, in particular the Act of Supremacy of 1534, Henry became the 'Supreme head of the Church of England'. Further Acts authorized the 'Dissolution of the Monasteries'. This took place between 1538 and 1547, the year of Henry's death.

The Dissolution of the Monasteries

This was a major event during these turbulent times. Henry VIII carried out this major reform in two stages, starting with the smaller abbeys in 1536. Two years later this was extended to the large religious houses. While all this was going on the often rich and famous shrines in many cathedrals and abbeys were being stripped, and gold, silver and jewels were being carried off in wagonloads. Not all monasteries were completely destroyed – because of their remoteness several of the great abbeys in North Yorkshire remain as skeletons – but in the main total ruination was achieved, if only by the removal of lead roofs. It was the lead that was valuable; it was nearly always recycled, often finding its way into a new royal palace. Once the roof of a building was gone decay set in rapidly. Nevertheless, many former monastic buildings were converted to secular use, often becoming houses.

Today it is believed that some 700 religious buildings were affected by the Dissolution, and the religious orders to which these buildings belonged owned between them about a quarter of the whole country.

* * *

Things did not improve after Henry's death and the succession of his son Edward VI, who reigned from 1547 to 1553. On the king's behalf (he was only 9 when he ascended the throne) the Lord Protector, Edward Seymour, Duke of Somerset, pursued the speedy implementation of all things Protestant. The 1552 Prayer Book marked the establishment of Protestantism. Images, shrines, rood lofts and statues of saints were removed or broken, stained glass windows were smashed when they venerated saints, wallpaintings were covered over with whitewash and churches were provided with new pulpits. The Holy Communion table was substituted for the altar, and roods and their lofts were replaced by scriptural messages, and texts of the Lord's Prayer and the Commandments.

After Edward died in 1553 the throne went to his half-sister, Mary, daughter of Henry VIII and Catherine of Aragon, who, like her mother, was a devout Catholic. Mary, who sent a number of Protestant martyrs to be burned at the stake, declared the English church again Catholic, and churchwardens throughout the land reinstalled many of the church goods banned in the previous reign.

Mary died childless in 1558 at the age of 42 and her half sister, Elizabeth, who had been brought up a Protestant, acceded to the throne and repudiated papal supremacy. She suppressed the Mass and made England once more a Protestant state. She reigned for 44 years and died in 1603. We know that during her reign and that of her successor James I (1603–25) many of the remaining wallpaintings were covered with limewash and more shrines, tabernacles, rood lofts and statues of saints were removed. However, the forces opposed to Catholicism did not make themselves really violently felt again until the coming of Cromwell and the Commonwealth in the seventeenth century. In 1643 Parliament authorized a massive onslaught on 'superstitious images and inscriptions in churches throughout the land'. The Puritans were in control, and throughout the country parties went out to strip the churches of ornament. It was the stained glass in particular that faced the onslaught this time, especially during the Civil War (1642–9), when many churches were used as billets for Puritan troops. Today it is believed that the Puritan assault on church furnishings and interiors was far more severe than Henry VIII's assault on the abbeys. It is known that Cromwell's troops even used guns to remove items that could not be reached by any other means.

Needless to say during these years of political and religious instability very few new churches were built.

All this is pretty hard to follow for church explorers who are not well-versed in English history, because a lot of the violence against churches that is thought to have been carried out during the Reformation was in fact carried out a century later. There are two main things to remember about all this. The first is that if it were not for these two periods of extreme religious turbulence all our churches would look extremely different today and we should have no Church of England. The second is that the only extensive church building in the seventeenth century took place towards the end of the century.

After the Restoration of King Charles II in 1660 there was a natural desire for peace and stability. Some churches had been built in the new Classical style known as Palladian, named after an influential Italian architect – Andrea Palladio – who based his theories and designs on the architecture of ancient Rome. However, the serious rebuilding was not to start until after the Great Fire of London in 1666. The churches rebuilt by Sir Christopher Wren and his followers at this time set the pace for the style that was to become known as Baroque, and it could not

Ingestre, Staffordshire, 1676: Classical Revival.

have been more different from the pointed arches that character-ized the Gothic style. In total 51 of the churches of the City were rebuilt, and the influence of Wren in this part of London is every-where. Although this style was tremendously influential and new churches in this basic style were built in many towns and villages, there are few churches outside London like those in the City, with their distinctive and often very elaborate towers and spires.

By this time the Gothic style had all but disappeared and the Classical Revival was firmly established. Parish churches built during this period were generally simple in plan and classical in influence. There was usually a quite plain main block, containing nave and flanking aisles and often no chancel of the conventional type. This was a direct response to the demands that during these Protestant days the Book of Common Prayer should be supreme. These churches became known as 'auditory' churches because the emphasis was at all times on the Word.

The churches of this time usually took the form of a single large room. When there was a chancel it was small, with just an altar.

St Lawrence Jewry, City of London, 1671–7: Classical Revival.

The arch – if there was one – between this space and the nave was purely decorative, and not structural as it traditionally was in Gothic churches. Nearly always decoration gave way to plainness, grandeur to simplicity. In keeping with the spirit of the Enlightenment and the reaction against all that was mysterious, Gothic and Catholic, the windows in churches of this period were usually rectangular with square or round heads – anything but pointed – and had large areas of clear glass.

The eighteenth century

Church building got off to a rapid start in the eighteenth century because in 1711 Queen Anne introduced a new Act empowering the building of 50 new churches in London and the suburbs. These 'Queen Anne churches' are usually on large and spacious sites – totally different from the cramped medieval sites on which most of the city churches had been rebuilt.

Sadly only 12 were built, but they were a huge influence on the church building of the next few generations. As in the much smaller City churches, the hallmarks of these churches and their imitators were clean, open, broad spaces with clarity of vision and excellent woodwork, with ordered, unjumbled interiors and

*Remodelled elegance: the 18th-century interior of the medieval
All Saints, Chalbury, Dorset.*

a strong emphasis on the pulpit. Many had – and still have –
galleries. Externally they relied heavily on the ancient Classical
orders of architecture, exemplified by shallow pitched roofs and
columns on plinths. Think of the ancient Greek temples you have
seen – or seen photos of – and you can't miss churches built in this
style.

Outside the cities many country churches were remodelled,
with high-backed family pews and new three-decker pulpits, with
parson's prayer desk, seat for the parish clerk, high sounding
board and hour glass.

Sometimes this was positioned half way down the side of the
church. This was the age when the sermon dominated the pro-
ceedings and demanded the attention of the congregation for
hours on end. The altar was often encased in rails and a gallery
installed at the east end.

Although many church explorers are enchanted with the
rusticity, the mystery, and the sheer age of ancient churches, it is
easy to forget that of the 16,000 or so parish churches in England
and Wales less than 10,000 are medieval. Most of the remainder
have been built since 1700.

The nineteenth century

We think of this century as primarily the Victorian Age, but in fact Queen Victoria did not come onto the throne until 1837, and before the school of High Church Victorian architects really got going there was a Greek Revival period in which parish churches reflected the temples of ancient Greece.

The Greek Revival was at its height from about 1810 to 1830. Most of the churches built in this style are in cities. Probably the best known is All Souls, Langham Place, London. This is a John Nash church. Nash (1752-1835) was one of the Commissioners of the Church Building Act of 1818, which made provision for about 230 churches to be built using government money in industrial cities of the Midlands and North, in addition to London. This was a direct response by the government of the day to the fact that few churches had been built in the late years of the eighteenth century and the early years of the nineteenth, and the Industrial Revolution was in full flight.

Although some Gothic Revival churches date from the early 1820s the movement only really got going in earnest after 1841 when A. W. N. Pugin wrote his *Contrasts*. Pugin argued successfully that the only really Christian architecture was Gothic. Despite dying at the age of 40 he was hugely influential and his ideas were taken up enthusiastically by the Church of England, whose High Church or Tractarian Movement was just then bringing the gospel to the industrial slums. The result was the most prolific period of church building in English history.

Inside remodelled medieval churches the Victorian reformers replaced the box pews with open benches with free seats for all. Galleries were removed, screens and chancels raised up. Large areas of floor tiles were introduced and screens began once again to separate chancel from nave. Stained glass – much of it of high quality – was vastly overdone, with the result that many Victorian churches are so dark that it is hard to appreciate much of the quality of their interiors.

Much Victorian work can look mechanical and repetitive, because this was the age when new machines for all sorts of purposes were being invented and developed. The result is that many Victorian churches, especially in their window tracery and internal stonework, show obvious signs of hurried mass production. However, look carefully at the interiors of many Victorian churches and you will realize that this was also an age in which there was a great revival of craftsmanship, not only in stained glass work but in tiles, woodwork, metalwork and fabrics.

The second half of the nineteenth century was the age of the great suburban church. As working towns expanded churches were built to meet the needs of their communities.

The twentieth century

In many twentieth-century churches you can see the constant debate about whether a church should be contemporary – or timeless. It is always interesting to look at a twentieth-century church and try to guess the age to within ten years. Somehow buildings that experimented with new materials a few years ago have a habit of looking curiously old-fashioned 10 or 20 years on.

The ideas of simplicity and utility encompassed by the Arts and Crafts Movement, with its emphasis on traditional building methods and natural materials, found their way into churches like Brockhampton-by-Ross (1901/2) by W. R. Lethaby; St Mary, Great Warley, Essex (1904) by C. Harrison Townsend; St Andrew, Roker, Tyne & Wear (1906/7) by E. S. Prior; and St

A typical mid 20th-century parish church, St Mary, Headington, Oxfordshire, 1958.

Edward the Confessor at Kempley, Gloucestershire (1903) by Randall Wells.

At the same time churches like St Jude, Hampstead Garden Suburb (1910), by Sir Edwin Lutyens, were blends of these ideas plus some Classical and English vernacular influences.

With decreasing church attendance and vast increases in material and labour costs church architecture in the twentieth century was generally constrained by costs, although one would not necessarily think so looking at the Gothic interior of St Mary, Wellingborough. The architect was Sir J. Ninian Comper. Built during 1908–30, this was one of the last great churches in the Gothic tradition. Today it is considered far too costly to attempt to build churches in this style.

Rather later came St Wilfred's, Brighton (1933), by H. S. Goodhart-Rendell. Now converted into flats, it is still a fine building from the exterior.

Outstanding post-Second World War churches have included St Luke's, Milber, Devon (a suburb of Newton Abbott), by Adam Martin, completed in 1963; churches rebuilt after bomb damage, such as All Hallows-by-the-Tower and St Bride's, Fleet Street, in London, and the ecumenical church of Christ the Cornerstone, Milton Keynes completed in 1991. Churches like the one at Milton Keynes re-establish a link with the past in that they have a mixture of roles, combining the functions of church and meeting-place very effectively. The church of St Paul, Harringay, Greater London, opened in 1993, has a striking modern interior. The architect was Peter Jenkins.

Round churches

The church of the Holy Sepulchre in Jerusalmen, captured by Crusaders in 1099, became the model for round churches built all over Europe. In England five are still to be seen, of which the most famous is the Temple Church in London. The others are the Holy Sepulchre in Cambridge, St Sepulchre in Northampton, Little Maplestead in Essex and the chapel of Ludlow Castle in Shropshire. All date from the Norman or English Romanesque period.

PART 3

Inside the Church

PART I

Building the Church

4

Main Features

Generations have trod, have trod, have trod
Gerard Manley Hopkins

Our churches were deliberately built to inspire people. Their interiors were designed to stir the senses. Hundreds of years later it is still possible to walk into a fine old parish church and feel a sense of awe. Even hardened agnostics sometimes admit to walking into a church and feeling their senses taking over.

All sorts of people who visit old churches talk about the 'vibes' they emit. Somehow it is as if the walls give off a sort of holy radioactivity: one is aware that they have absorbed the feelings as well as the prayers of countless generations, who, whatever their beliefs, have been happy to kneel down and express their hopes and fears, joys and sadnesses, to God.

Over the centuries the old church has represented a linchpin to these people, who have found God to be real to them when they are inside. By just being there the building still performs that function. And just as ever, the walls are still absorbing the prayers and feelings of people who are prepared to come in and pray – whatever the current state of their religious beliefs – for their fellow human beings.

If the interiors of most historic parish churches could be returned overnight to what they looked like 600 years ago, parishioners entering the next day would find it difficult, at first, to recognize they were in the same building. This may seem a huge exaggeration, but consider what church interiors were like when the Church reigned supreme.

The inside was bright and colourful. True, there would have been dark and gloomy corners in the larger churches where parishioners could say their rosaries at side altars such as the ones many of us associate with churches in Catholic countries such as Ireland or France. But the often gaudy colours of the wallpaintings were everywhere to be seen.

1. East window	11. Pulpit
2. High altar	12. Hymn board
3. Cross	13. Crucifix
4. Credence table	14. Banner
5. Sedilia	15. Lady chapel
6. Organ	16. Lectern
7. Altar rails	17. Pews
8. Chancel	18. Nave
9. Choir stalls	19. Font
10. Chancel step	20. Memorial brass

Inside the church: main features.

Early (c1300) wall-painting from the church of St Lawrence, Little Wenham, Suffolk. Images of Ss Margaret, Catherine and Mary Magdalene are part of an important set on the east wall. Photo by Boris Baggs, courtesy The Churches Conservation Trust.

These paintings covered all manner of subjects – from the lives of the saints and scenes from the Scriptures to a large, rather lumbering St Christopher, carrying the Christ child on his shoulders (a very common motif), to scenes in the life of Our Lady.

In addition to this nobody who has seen a version of the medieval doom, or last judgement, indicating in vivid form the fates of the saved and the damned, will readily forget the experience. These amazing wallpaintings, of which about 70 still exist in part or whole, were designed to instil fear and obedience among the illiterate masses that worshipped there.

All the windows would have been filled with stained glass depicting the saints and their legends, and throughout the church there would be pictures and images of Our Lady and the saints. For this reason the twinkle of candles would have been everywhere.

In addition to this, much of the stonework on the arches and pillars would probably have been brightly painted – many samples of this practice remain – and the woodwork of screens,

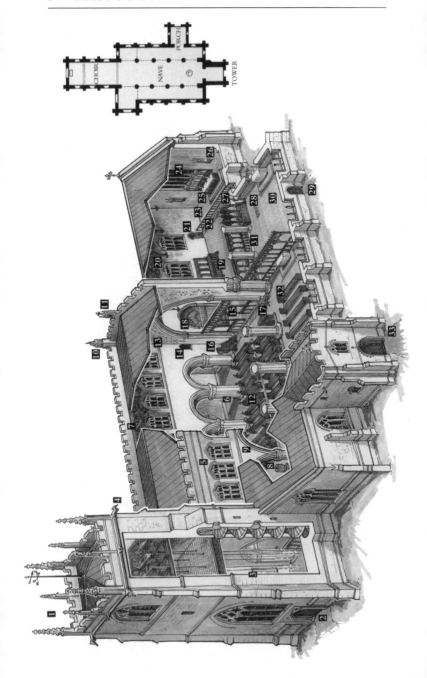

Tower

1. 15th-century additions to 14th-century tower
2. 15th-century west door
3. Bellringers mementoes
4. Gargoyle or water spout

Nave

5. 15th-century Perpendicular clearstory
6. 12th-century Transitional arcade
7. Arch-braced tie-beam roof
8. Norman font
9. Late 13th-century arcade
10. Boiler flue, 19th century
11. Sanctus bell
12. Pews
13. Doom painting
14. Door to former rood loft
15. Rood screen
16. Pulpit
17. Lectern

Chancel

18. Organ
19. Choir and stalls
20. Hammer-beam roof
21. Door to vestry
22. Communion rail
23. Sanctuary
24. 15th-century perpendicular east window
25. Altar
26. Piscina
27. Squint
28. Tomb
29. Priest's door
30. Late 14th-century chancel
31. Parclose screen

Aisle

32. 14th-century seating in Decorated south aisle

Porch

33. 15th-century additions to Decorated porch

Cutaway diagram of a large Perpendicular parish church, built in several phases.

doors and roofs would have been richly carved, painted and gilded.

Visually then, the scene on entering the church would initially have been that of a large, pewless, often rather mysterious space, on account of all the stained glass windows, with flickering candles casting light and shadow upon the vast picture book that was the walls. This would be quite alien to our modern tastes, which prefer our churches to emphasize the beauty and plainness of the stone and to contrast this with the tasteful blend of colours in the glass in the windows.

In medieval times the church would also have been a far busier place than it is today. Apart from on Sundays, when just about everyone would go to church, the building would be totally different in the week from the rather quiet and often unused place most of us expect to see when we visit.

The large, open main body of the building would have been used in much the same way as we use a village hall or social club. People would talk and trade and hold meetings (at Aldeburgh in Suffolk it is said that ship auctions were held in the nave) while at the side altars priests would have been saying Masses.

We know from the dog doors to be found that animals wandered around, and as all sorts of trading was carried out in the churchyard there is no reason to doubt that these activities extended to the inside of the church. After all, in early medieval times life was much more jumbled up: there were far fewer buildings attached to specific functions and perhaps above all parish government and local civil administration were still one and the same thing. The church was very much the centre of community life.

So no wonder there were no pews in the nave: the sacred and the secular was far more intermixed. Peace and quiet prevailed only in the chancel – and, hopefully, at the numerous side altars. We know they vastly exceeded those of today from the piscinas that remain. These are wall niches that performed much the same role as a basin when the priest washed his hands at Mass. It easy to forget that all this was before the time of Henry VIII, the Reformation and the beginning of the Anglican Church.

Despite all this, if you were to enter the church, as most people still do, through the south porch, the basic shape of the church would probably look much as it does today.

If it is in the shape of a cross – a cruciform church – the symbolism is obvious. With other shapes of church it is less so, but all churches are full of symbolism.

The font

You will probably next encounter the font. This is traditionally positioned by the door because this is the point of entry to the Christian faith. If the font is not by the south door – the usual place of entry – then it will probably be by the west door, if there is one, in an area known as the baptistery.

Fonts are where baptism takes place. It is an event that is deeply symbolic for Christians because it represents the admission of a child or adult into the Christian community and the casting away of evil.

In the past the basin of the font contained baptismal water, which traditionally changed only twice a year, at Easter and Whitsun, when it was solemnly blessed. A result of this was the practice of removing holy water for 'medical' and more sinister practices. So in the thirteenth century an ecclesiastical statute was

Twelfth-century, highly carved font at Eardisley, Hereford.

The famous medieval wooden font cover at Ufford, Suffolk.

introduced that required all fonts to have lockable covers. You can still see the remains of this in the form of abrasions in the stone on many historic fonts. Sometimes the font covers remain and are very elaborate, as at Ufford and Sudbury in Suffolk, Salle in Norfolk and Swimbridge in Devon.

Font covers like this take the form of a wooden canopy, rising above like a church steeple and descending by means of a system of pulleys. They are very easy to handle as there is a counter-weight. They might be brightly painted, in which case the work was probably carried out by Victorian restorers who were keen on reproducing what they thought were the medieval colours.

In many churches the ancient font has survived, even if those churches have lost all other traces of their medieval origins. It therefore follows that the font is sometimes a most effective guide to the age of a church.

What to look out for

Fonts are enormously varied. *Saxon* fonts are invariably stone and are usually known as 'drum fonts'. They are usually lined with lead, stepped at the base and decorated with crude but vigorous motifs such as arcading and cable mouldings.

Saxon font, Deerhurst, Gloucestershire.

Saxon fonts are to be found at:

Cornwall: Egloshayle
Devon: Dolton
Dorset: Melbury Bubb
Gloucestershire: Deerhurst
Hampshire: Anstey
Northamptonshire: Little Billing
Warwickshire: Curdworth
Wiltshire: Potterne

Norman

Norman fonts are very numerous – there are reckoned to be at least 100 in Devon alone – and invariably massive, often adorned with carvings of monsters and figures with amazingly varied origins, from Celtic motifs to Scandinavian and eastern folklore.

Norman font,
Cowley,
Gloucestershire.

Here are a few fine examples of Norman, or English Romanesque, fonts:

Buckinghamshire: Aylesbury, Bledlow, Pitstone
Cornwall: Bodmin, Morwenstow
Cumbria: Bridekirk
Derbyshire: Tissington, Whitwell, Youlgreave
Devon: Exeter (St Mary Steps), Harberton, Hartland, Highampton, Instow, Jacobstowe, Kenn, Loddiswell, Luppitt, Lustleigh, Lydford, Marystow, Sheepwash, South Brent, Spreyton
Glamorgan: St Donats
Herefordshire: Castle Frome, Eardisley
Monmouthshire: Abergavenny
Norfolk: Breckles, Burnham Deepdale, Shernborne
Oxfordshire: Hook Norton
Shropshire: Cound
Somerset: Locking
Suffolk: Kettlebaston, Preston St Mary
Warwickshire: Coleshill
Wiltshire: Avebury
Worcestershire: Chaddesley Corbett
Yorkshire: Cowlam, Grimston, Langtoft, Kirkburn, Reighton, Thorpe Salvin

Early English

Early English fonts are often characterized by having their bowls supported on a circular shaft with four detached shafts at the angles. Eaton Bray and Studham, both in Bedfordshire, have finely carved stone fonts in this style. In Essex there are fonts of this style at Springfield and Fryerning. Fonts of this type with detached shafts are often called 'Purbeck fonts' because their bowls were frequently made from Purbeck marble.

Early English font, Lackford, Suffolk.

Fourteenth-century font with oak cover, dating from the late seventeenth century

Decorated

Fonts of this period (*c.*1300–50) are relatively few, probably due to the ample numbers that were created during the Norman and Early English periods. Many fonts retain their bowls of Purbeck marble, but they are often set on newer stems. During this period bowls tended to become polygonal – usually octagonal – with deeply incised carvings, often reflecting window tracery. Good examples are at Finchingfield in Essex, Faringdon in Oxfordshire, and Brailes in Warwickshire.

Perpendicular

This was the period in which the font reached its highest development. Perpendicular fonts are elaborately decorated, though sadly many suffered great damage at the hands of Cromwell's men, who took delight in hacking away the images.

Perpendicular font, Crowle, Worcestershire.

If you are travelling in East Anglia look out for Seven-Sacrament fonts. These show the seven sacraments of the Church on seven of the panels of the bowl, and usually the baptism of Our Lord or the Crucifixion on the remaining panel.

The sacraments are: Baptism; Confirmation; Mass, Eucharist or Communion; Penance or Confession; Holy Orders; Holy Matrimony; and Unction or anointing of the sick. There are 25 such fonts in Norfolk and 13 in Suffolk and only 2 elsewhere – at Farningham in Kent and Nettlecombe in Somerset.

The other type to look out for is the panelled stone font, in which the symbols of the four evangelists are usually portrayed alternating with angels holding musical instruments, or shields, or carved lions. As with Seven Sacrament fonts this type is particularly common in Norfolk. Good examples are at Acle, Happisburgh and Horsham St Faith, and Chediston, Saxmundham, and Stoke-by-Nayland in Suffolk

Lead

Lead fonts are rare. There are only about 40 in churches in England. Most are Norman or date from soon after. They are to be found at (among other places) Ashover in Derbyshire, Penn in Buckinghamshire, Burghill in Herefordshire, Brookland in Kent, Frampton-on-Severn, Sandhurst and Tidenham in Gloucestershire, Brundall in Norfolk, and Dorchester Abbey and Long Wittenham, both in Oxfordshire.

Post-Reformation

After the Reformation the sacraments became very much less important in Protestant Britain. However, the sacrament of Baptism continued to be required within the established church, as well as in most Nonconformist churches.

A fine post-Reformation font, St Vedast, City of London.

Many fonts which had become damaged or dated were turned out of the church, to be replaced by new ones. This is why to this day we hear of ancient stone fonts being found in odd corners of villages and returned to the parish church.

During the Reformation many congregations plastered over the carved panels of their old stone fonts as a form of disguise so that they were spared from destruction. With the beginning of church building again in the late seventeenth and eighteenth centuries, new fonts took on totally different, Classical designs. The bowls were usually small and their pedestals finely turned – totally different from the massive stone fonts found in Gothic churches.

Good examples of 'slim line' fonts of this sort are to be seen in the churches of the City of London.

You will also find examples of 'slim line' fonts at the following churches with eighteenth-century interiors:

Bedfordshire: Cardington
Buckinghamshire: West Wycombe
Dorset: Chalbury
Essex: Billericay, Lambourne End
Hertfordshire: Essendon
Oxfordshire: Chislehampton
Sussex: Warminghurst
Worcestershire: Great Witley

Font oddities

'Font projections' occur when the font has a small subsidiary bowl either marked off by a division inside the main bowl or attached to it. They are thought to have been been receptacles or ledges for books, holy oil, candles and other items required by the priest at Baptism.

Examples are to be seen at:

Derbyshire: Youlgreave
Devon: Feniton
Gloucestershire: Rudford
Greater London: Rainham

At Rothbury in Northumberland the post-Reformation font of 1664 sits on a beautifully carved ninth-century Saxon shaft.

Wooden fonts are extremely rare, but there is one at Marks Tey, Essex. It is of oak and dates from the fifteenth century. A later wooden font, in the form of a fluted wooden pillar, can be seen at Gayhurst, Buckinghamshire.

At Cranbrook, Kent, there is a font designed for full adult immersion. It dates from 1710 and looks like an upright coffin.

The nave

This is the main body of the church, where most of the congregation stood and worshipped in medieval times. If you should spot a stone ledge around the outer wall take note: in many churches a

A splendid nave in the Perpendicular style of the later 14th century, Walpole St Peter, Norfolk. (Photo: Richard Tilbrook)

A most unusual – in fact unique in an English church – sciapod bench end. A sciapod is a strange creature from the world of folklore that rests under the shade of his large foot. St Mary, Dennington, Suffolk.

stone ledge was sometimes provided so the elderly and infirm could 'go to the wall' to rest. This is the meaning of the modern expression. The word nave is Latin and means 'ship'. Again this is highly symbolic: in past times a ship was often used as a symbol for the Church, carrying Christians through the frequently rough seas of life.

The main worshippers in a service still congregate in the nave, but they would find it strange if there were no seats. However, this is how it was in the past. Seating, in the form of primitive benches, only appeared in churches around the end of the thirteenth century. The majority of carved benches in England date from the second half of the fifteenth century and after.

Wooden seats are correctly termed *benches* and not pews. The word pew really means elevated, or enclosed, seating.

Ancient 'poppy head' bench ends in an East Anglian parish church.

Early church benches often have wonderfully carved *bench ends*. These are one of the great glories of English parish churches, and no church explorers should fail to notice them. It is easy to notice the high quality carving in the *poppy head* or other motif at the top of the pew and omit to look at the carved panels in their sides, particularly if the church is a dark one or is unlit. These side panels are often a wonderful riot of carvings. Popular motifs include animals, saints, figures from folklore, fertility symbols, mermaids, ships, windmills, hunting scenes and grotesques of all types, all standing next to figures of the saints or Instruments of the Passion. The old churches of the West Country are rich hunting grounds for these, but you are far more likely to see poppy heads, which usually (but not always) resemble a fleur-de-lys in form, in East Anglia, the other area famed for its bench ends. In addition to panels in the ends of benches, old churches in East Anglia often have delightful carvings of human figures, beasts or birds placed just below the poppy heads on the corners of the bench ends. In the panelling, there are generally fewer quaint and grotesque figures than in the West Country.

Ancient high-quality carved bench ends can be seen at:

Bedfordshire: Willington
Cambridgeshire: Fen Ditton
Cornwall: Altarnun, Cardinham, Kilkhampton, Morwenstow
Devon: Abbotsham, Braunton, Cadbury, East Budleigh, Marwood
Leicestershire: Dunton Bassett, Gaddesby
Norfolk: Feltwell, Harpley, Upper Sheringham, Wiggenhall
Northamptonshire: Finedon
Oxfordshire: Minster Lovell
Somerset: Bishop's Lydeard, Broomfield, Clapton-in-Gordano, Crowcombe, Lapford, Milverton, Monksilver, Spaxton, Stogursey, Worle
Suffolk: Blythburgh, Dennington, Fressingfield, Ufford
Surrey: Dunsfold
Worcestershire: Eckington

Box pews

These are large, high-sided family pews that were often heated on winter days. They are a great curiosity for many who do not regularly explore old churches, but are not as rare as you might think. They date mostly from the seventeenth and eighteenth centuries, when the emphasis of worship changed to the reading desk and pulpit as the focus of attention and seating was arranged accordingly, with the best views reserved for those in family pews. These large family pews were usually reserved for the squire and other grand families of the parish. So in the seventeenth and

Grand family pew: the province of one of the foremost families in the parish, Kirkby Malham, Yorkshire.

eighteenth centuries the order of seating in parish churches reflected a rigid social structure, which was undoubtedly one of the things that drove many worshippers to the competing Nonconformist chapels.

Pew Renting was also common at this time. The rents were paid to the churchwardens, who used the money for church maintenance. If you could not afford to rent a pew then you were often accommodated in the *gallery*. In the eighteenth and nineteenth centuries galleries were regularly installed in parish churches. Today they are regarded as something of a curiosity.

If you are a church furnishings enthusiast you will also be interested in pews with roofs. These became fashionable in the seventeenth century. They were supported on posts, rather similar to those of four poster beds. Some, like those at Croft and Wensley in Yorkshire, and at Langley Marish in Berkshire, are elevated and very grand.

Where to see box pews (also known as family pews and parlour pews):

Berkshire: Langley Marish
Buckinghamshire: Lower Winchenden
Derbyshire: Castleton, Foremark
Devon: Colebrooke, Molland
Dorset: Chalbury, Winterborne Tomson
Durham: Croft-on-Tees
Essex: North End
Gloucestershire: Little Washbourne
Gwynedd: Llanengan
Herefordshire: Bishop's Castle
Hertfordshire: Stanstead Abbots
Lancashire: Whalley
Leicestershire: Staunton Harold
Middlesex: Stanmore
Norfolk: Melton Constable, Tibenham, Worstead
Northamptonshire: Cottesbrooke
Oxfordshire: Chislehampton, Rycote
Shropshire: Stokesay
Staffordshire: Broughton
Suffolk: Dennington, Gislingham, Heveningham, Kedington, Ramsholt, Tunstall
Sussex: West Grinstead
Wiltshire: Old Dilton
Yorkshire: Kirkby Malham, Wensley, Whitby

Other fine woodwork

Much of this is often to be found in the chancel, the area of the church that lies to the east of the nave and is usually divided from the nave by a screen or some other clear form of demarcation.

The chancels of many old parish churches had wooden stalls. These are different from the benches in the nave because of both their position and their styling. They are usually far grander, and

Misericord and fine carvings on the arms of stalls in a medieval parish church, St Peter and St Paul, Salle, Norfolk.

are separated from one another by projecting arms. They also often have elaborate carved canopies. Stalls are usually placed against the north and south walls and are often set against the back of the screen in order to face the altar. The stall ends nearly always have poppy heads, but are usually more elaborate than those of the nave bench ends.

When an old church has stalls in the chancel always look beneath for *misericords*. These are the hinged wooden seats which tip up to present a small projection beneath for the user to rest on when in a standing position. They were designed to provide support for the monks or canons who were able to rest without sitting during the interminable offices they had to attend every day. The design of misericords also ensured the monks would wake up if they nodded off and slumped down!

The presence of misericords implies that the church was once monastic, or could have been a collegiate church, with a small community of priests that was not tied to any major religious house or monastic rule. This is an interesting point for the church explorer, because stalls with misericords are also sometimes found in more minor churches. When you find this it is quite probable that they have been imported from some other, larger church that either discarded them or more probably disappeared or was greatly reduced during the Dissolution of the Monasteries.

Apart from the splendid carving that usually adorns the stalls above, the undersides of the seats are nearly always carved

Fifteenth-century misericords in the choir, Sherborne Abbey, Dorset.

with a huge variety of subjects ranging through mythology, medieval romances, day-to-day village scenes, the faces of ancients, jesters and suffering husbands and wives, sacred symbols, birds, beasts and fishes, plus mythical figures and Christian allusions. In all this, symbolism again looms large. For instance, Sampson carrying off the gates of Gaza is associated with the Resurrection, while the pelican, which often occurs, represents Christ.

While the carvings on the undersides of misericords can be appreciated by anyone for their skill, humour and humanity, their full meaning will only be understood by the few who take the trouble to learn their 'language' .

Large numbers of misericords remain. They range in age from the late thirteenth century to about the mid-fourteenth century. There is a set in most medieval cathedrals.

In parish churches fine examples are to be found at:

Cheshire: Nantwich
Cumbria: Cartmel Priory
Dorset: Christchurch Priory, Sherborne Abbey
Kent: Minster-in-Thanet
Lancashire: Whalley
Lincolnshire: Boston
Northamptonshire: Higham Ferrers
Shropshire: Ludlow
Somerset: Worle
Warwickshire: Stratford-upon-Avon
Worcestershire: Great Malvern Priory, Ripple
Yorkshire: Beverley, York (The Minster and St Mary)

Floors and floor tiles

As you walk through the church be sure to take note of the floor. Apart from observing any inscriptions and brasses – also places where brasses have been placed and removed – the key thing for the church explorer is to know if it is an interesting one or not. In many cases church floors were replaced with rather bland pine boarding and patterned coloured clay tiles in the chancel, which are not of much interest.

But it is good to have an eye for the genuine medieval tiles. These can be plain clay, in which case they are usually small, square, orange in colour and 'chunky'. They can also be encaustic, which means they have a pattern set in them in coloured clays that were fired at the same time as the 'main' tile. The Victorians also used this technique, but in a more mechanized way. You can tell genuine medieval encaustic floor tiles: they usually look very worn and very ancient. There are small areas of them in many

Medieval floor tiles are still to be found in many parish churches. They may be plain, or if patterned were formed by inserting clay of a different colour into the base clay before firing and are known as encaustic tiles. Both are to be seen here at St Mary, Charlton-on-Otmoor, Oxfordshire.

ancient churches – often rather uneven – but very good examples are few and far between. The best counties for them are Devon and Worcestershire. The ones at the tiny church in Hailes, Gloucestershire, are also very fine. In East Anglia you will find many fine floors of clay pamments. These are quite thick clay tiles. They look wonderful when matured by the patina of time. They vary in colour from cream to a deep orange. Occasionally very dark ones can also be seen.

Pulpits

A pulpit is an elevated platform from which the priest preaches his or her sermon. In some churches readings also take place from here. The pulpit usually stands beside the chancel arch, the arch that separates the nave from the priest's end of the church or chancel. In the early medieval period sermons were rare: the earliest sermons date from the mid-1300s

Medieval pulpits were made of stone or oak, and the finest ones are of the elegant 'wineglass' kind, with a slender stem and a drum-shaped preaching box.

After the Reformation (see pages 80–2) the Church changed many of its attitudes and practices. The split with Rome brought about a much greater emphasis on communication between the priest and his congregation, and the pulpit acquired a more central role in worship. So did the reading desk, or reading pew, from which the priest conducted the services.

*A fine Classical pulpit with sounding board, St Mary
Woolnoth, Lombard Street, London.*

Pre-Reformation pulpits

Most pulpits from this age date from the 1400s and early 1500s.
They are mainly wooden and most are found in Devon and
Norfolk churches.

Fine examples of pre-Reformation pulpits are to be found at:

Devon: Chivelstone, Coldridge, East Allington, Halberton, Holne, Ipplepen, Kenton
Norfolk: Burnham Norton, Castle Acre, Horsham St Faith, North Walsham, South Burlingham, South Creake

There are also fine pre-Reformation pulpits at Long Sutton, Monksilver and Trull, all in Somerset.

Fine pre-Reformation stone pulpits can be found at:

Devon: Bovey Tracey, Chittlehampton, Dartmouth (St Saviour), Dittisham
Gloucestershire: Chedworth, Cirencester, Northleach
Somerset: Banwell, Bleadon, Hutton
Staffordshire: Wolverhampton (St Peter)

Pulpit oddities

The oldest known pulpit in England, at Mellor, Greater Manchester, dates from the 1300s and is hewn out of a solid piece of rock.

There is a pulpit on wheels at St Mary the Great, Cambridge, and a similar arrangement on a sliding track at St John Baptist, Hoxton, London.

A *frater pulpit* is a raised lectern or balcony set in the wall in former monastic churches. From here passages of Scripture were read during meals. At Beaulieu Abbey in Hampshire the frater pulpit is still in use in what is now the parish church.

Lecterns

Lecterns are simply bookstands from which the priest or his or her nominee reads the Scriptures, and sometime preaches. However, like pulpits there are many kinds. The most striking are

A fine contemporary lectern, St Augustine, Darlington.

the eagle lecterns, in either brass or wood (usually carved oak). Again, symbolism looms large: the eagle symbolizes the carrying of the gospel to the four corners of the earth. It was considered in days gone by to be the bird which soared highest in the sky, and therefore nearest to heaven. Many eagle lecterns have dragons at the foot of the pillar, symbolizing the evil powers conquered by the Word of God.

Unusual lecterns

At Oxborough in Norfolk the fifteenth-century brass eagle lectern dates from before the Reformation and is one of a small number of lecterns known as 'Peter's Pence' lecterns. There are 12 pre-Reformation eagle lecterns in Norfolk and 3 in Suffolk. Peter's Pence lecterns are so called because they were previously used to take coins for the annual tax known by this name levied to support the See of Rome. The coins were pushed into slots on either side of the eagle's beak and collected via a larger slot in the tail.

The oldest known lecterns are of stone and date from around 1200. There is one at Norton in Worcestershire, which was dug up in 1813 in the churchyard at Evesham Abbey. There is another at Crowle in the same county, in a similar limestone and again found in a churchyard by a Victorian antiquarian. There is another stone lectern of similar age – this time of marble – at Much Wenlock, Shropshire. At Crich and Etwall in Derbyshire, ancient stone lecterns are built into the north wall of the chancel.

At High Bray in North Devon there is an unusual lectern – an angel supporting a bookplate on his wings.

At Monksilver in Somerset the lectern has no stand or column: instead, the eagle book-rest is fixed to the screen by an iron support and is made to swivel round.

At Ranworth in the Norfolk Broads the fifteenth-century double-sided oak lectern is two reading desks at different levels – one for the Bible and the other for a large book for singing from. There is also a double-sided lectern – in brass and dating from the nineteenth century – at Stansted Mountfitchet in Essex.

The lectern usually stands in front of the screen, if there is one (for screens see pages 140–6) which is usually beneath the *chancel arch*. This leads to the chancel – the main section of the church to the east of the nave.

At this point of your tour you may also spot the ancient *squint*, or *hagioscope*, if there is one. This is an aperture cut through the wall of the chancel arch (see page 174).

The altar

The altar is the focal point of the church. It is regarded as the holy heart of the church because this is the place where Mass is celebrated. For Catholics, both Anglican and Roman, the celebration of the Mass is the chief purpose of any church.

Ancient stone altar, or mensa, surmounting a wooden communion table, St Faith, Farmcote, Gloucestershire.

Christians of a more Protestant inclination would disagree, which is why the altar has so many other names – 'The Holy Table', 'The Lord's Table' and 'God's Board' to name but three.

Before the Reformation the altar was a stone structure, but the whole idea of sacrifice, for the Reformers, was alien to their way of thinking. Stone altars went out of the churches for this reason; wooden tables took their place.

Today in an Anglican church with a strong Protestant leaning you are far more likely to see a wooden table than a stone altar. In contrast, if a stone altar were to be dug up in the churchyard of a church with a strong Anglo-Catholic tradition (and this is still happening from time to time) there is little doubt that the congregation would welcome its reinstatement in the sanctuary.

Fine contemporary stone altar, St Thomas, Huddersfield.

An altar is basically a simple table, but the significances
attached to it are anything but simple, and of all the elements that
make up the interior of a church the altar has, over the years,
probably been the subject of more heated theological and liturgi-
cal debate than any other.

The *mensa* (*Latin: table*) is the stone top of such altars. It is always marked with five small crosses, one at each corner and one at the centre, which were anointed by the consecrating bishop and which stood for the five wounds of Christ. You will find it hard to see all these in a church with a stone altar today, because they are usually railed off and covered with embroidered cloths, frontals and side curtains.

The Reformers of the mid-seventeenth century believed that the sacrifice of the Mass was heretical, and that to commemorate the Lord's Supper an ordinary table of wood should be used. So old stone altars were once again cast aside, often to be rediscovered later buried in the graveyard. The Reformed Church decreed that wooden Communion tables should be carried down to the entrance of the chancel, or into the nave, for the purposes of Holy Communion, or placed lengthwise in the chancel.

After this they were carried back to the sanctuary for storage. A few were made portable by having detachable staves, and one or two of these survive.

Shrines and places of pilgrimage

Some rare pieces of internal stonework had a small hollow fashioned in them to house the relic of a saint. This was a shrine. The relic was usually placed in a container called a reliquary, which was usually positioned in a cavity known as a confessio, which was usually sealed or closed with a thin stone. At the church of St Wite, Whitchurch Canonicorum in Dorset, there is a rare survival – a stone altar in the north transept with three holes in it. Into these, pilgrims in search of a cure would thrust their limbs. When in 1900 the casket behind was broken open, the bones of a small woman were found. St Wite or Candida was a Celtic female saint.

Larger shrines

Shrines are elaborate tombs that house the remains of a saint. In medieval times such tombs were places of healing, protection, forgiveness and spiritual guidance. Pilgrimages to the shrines of such saints became the medieval equivalent of modern holidays.

From time to time you will still see a *watching loft* above an

Medieval shrine of St Edburg, St Michael's, Stanton Harcourt, Oxfordshire.

ancient shrine. These were observation posts, usually directly above the shrine, from which a vigil could be kept to prevent sacrilege or theft.

Not all shrines were located in major churches. Although the well-known Anglican ones are today housed in cathedrals, there were many in small country churches. We probably know of only a handful of these today, like the church of the nativity of the Blessed Virgin Mary at Madley, Herefordshire, where the shrine was housed in the crypt. At Stanton Harcourt in Oxfordshire the medieval shrine of St Edburg can be seen in St Michael's church.

The remains of shrines, or hints of where they stood, are again one of those things church explorers should be on the lookout for, because almost certainly shrines would have been common in many churches in early medieval times when cults of saints attracted pilgrims from far afield.

Today it is hard for many to understand how important pilgrimages were. They took place all over Europe, and to the well-known shrines at cathedrals and larger churches in this country. But there were also smaller shrines, where the bones or relics of saints and other venerated figures were said to lie. We know from Chaucer's *Canterbury Tales* that many going on these pilgrimages just regarded them as a holiday, but many people were sent on pilgrimages as penances, to attempt to make good a sin they had committed. Others went to curative shrines in search of a cure for ailments and diseases.

Unusual altars

At Great Milton, Oxfordshire, there is a very rare survival of a medieval portable stone altar. It measures only 9½ by 6½ inches and is set in the wooden top of a modern altar in the north aisle of the nave.

At Cleobury Mortimer church in Shropshire a portable seventeenth-century altar with staves has survived.

Altar rails

Most of these are post-Reformation. As the screens and rood lofts were pulled down these began to appear.

They are usually associated with William Laud, who was

Archbishop of Canterbury for 12 years (1633–45) during the reign of King Charles I. Laud wished to reform the English Church in a way compatible with Protestantism yet without giving way to some of the demands of the more extreme Puritanical elements of Protestantism. He was strongly opposed to the Puritan practice of moving the altar to the nave of the church for the purposes of the Communion service and fought to have altars placed at the east end of the chancel with an enclosing rail round them. This is why most altar rails in old churches date from this time or slightly after.

Fine Classical reredos – the carved screen behind the altar: St Thomas of Canterbury, Salisbury. This one dates from 1724.

The altar is the focal point of the *sanctuary*, which is the area behind the altar rails at the extreme east end of the church. The sanctuary is approached via the *chancel*, which is the area, usually divided by a screen or some other clear form of demarcation, that lies to the east of the nave and the transepts, if there are any. Inside the sanctuary, as well as the altar you will probably find a *piscina*, and probably *sedilia* (stone seats) if the church is an ancient one. Piscinas are stone bowls or drains, usually built into the south wall near the altar. Most piscinas beside high altars have a stone canopy, and drain directly onto the consecrated ground outside the walls of the church. In some churches you will find *double piscinas* – one for the washing of hands and the other for the sacred vessels. If you find a piscina somewhere in a church – perhaps in a transept – and there is no altar, this almost certainly indicates there was an altar there before.

At the rear of the altar there may well be a *reredos*, a decorated or carved screen or wallcovering. Most old stone reredoses have vanished or been badly defaced. Doubtless the Reformers, who were ordered to break up the altars, or the later Puritans would think it also part of their business to break off the heads of the 'superstitious images' behind it. In their place you might find a *retable*, or altarpiece in wood or fabric, or a painting.

Alternatively there might be painted wooden panels, or curtains, known as *riddells* and supported at the sides by often elaborate *riddell posts*

Crypts and undercrofts

These are fascinating for any church explorer who wants to do some real detective work, though if you really get into the subject your travels might take you to as many research libraries as ancient churches. There is an awful lot of confusion as to what a

The Anglo-Saxon crypt at All Saints Church, Wing, Buckinghamshire.

*The medieval undercroft chapel of All Souls, St Alphege, Solihull,
West Midlands.*

crypt really is, and which underground chambers in historic
churches really are crypts, and which are not.

From the times of the early Church, Christians, highly influenced by the Gospel stories of Jesus, believed that God could
work miracles of healing through the bones of saints or articles
which had been in contact with them. The graves of these early
saints, therefore, provided a location for such healing.

They also gave rise to cults. By the early Middle Ages the cult of
the saints, their relics and miracles grew at a great rate and provided good business for people like pardoners, who were licensed
by the Pope to sell indulgences, or forms of forgiveness for sins
that had been committed.

There seems little doubt that the sites of some of these holy
men's graves gave rise to some early churches and that the first
crypts were simple subterranean caverns beside or above the
grave of such a saint. We also know that sometimes it was easier

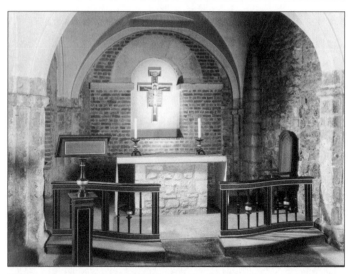

St Mary-le-Bow, Cheapside. The crypt of 1087 is in regular use as the Chapel of the Holy Spirit.

to exhume the graves of saints and martyrs and take their remains to a church to be venerated, where a crypt was created for this purpose.

Bearing in mind the number of ancient and often obscure saints, we can therefore hazard a guess that while truly ancient crypts are now a great rarity, before the Norman Conquest they must have been a great deal more common.

From time to time you also see clear signs of walled-up former subterranean chambers beneath the east end of ancient churches built on a slope. When these churches are known to be of Saxon origin then it seems fair to assume that any chambers beneath, as in the case of the small church of St Michael, at Duntisbourne Rouse, Gloucestershire (see page 3), were originally crypts. In the case of Duntisbourne Rouse very little more seems to be known about this small lower chamber, which is intact and readily accessible to visitors.

Very often these walled-up chambers were simply bone holes, otherwise known as charnel houses. After centuries of burials the

Walled-up subterranean chamber at St Mary,
Shipton-under-Wychwood, Oxfordshire.

parish graveyard to the south of the church would become full of the uncoffined dead and, in order to make room for future burials, the earth was turned over and the disturbed bones placed in a small chamber, usually beneath the church.

After hundreds of years it is often very hard to tell whether this chamber had been used as a crypt, dedicated to the memory of a local saint or martyr, in previous times. That is why the chamber beneath the chancel of the church of St Peter and St Giles at Sidbury, Devon, is still a mystery. It was discovered in 1898 and is on a slightly different axis to the previous Saxon church. There is little doubt that it predates the present twelfth-century chancel, but was it created specifically as a chamber used to venerate the remains of a local saint or martyr? And was it later used as a bone hole? We shall probably never know. There is a similarly mysterious chamber beneath the south aisle at Holy Trinity church, Rothwell, Northamptonshire. It is a much larger affair – 30 feet long – and it contains a huge collection of bones unearthed from the churchyard at different times.

Another famous bone hole or ossuary is beneath the chancel at St Leonard's at Hythe, Kent, and is again something entirely different. Originally it was not a crypt but a vaulted procession path created when the chancel was extended eastwards to the churchyard wall in the thirteenth century and it was no longer possible for outside processions to pass round the eastern end of the building. The bone hole at Hythe is opened regularly to the public, but the one at Rothwell has very limited opening.

All this is very different from an undercroft, which in this country is really a later development of the form of 'crypt' idea that had its beginning in Rome and took rather a long time to find its way across the channel. The best examples are to be seen in Italy and France and they are best defined as chambers, accessed by steps to either side, beneath the chancels and sanctuaries of churches built as chapels to venerate the remains of a martyr or patron or saint. The idea was taken up by the Victorians, who were fond of building apses (semicircular recesses) at the eastern extremity of a deliberately raised chancel, beneath which was a vaulted undercroft. The design followed that of the basilica church, an early form that took its pattern from ancient Rome.

The undercroft beneath the chantry chapel of St Alphege in the parish church at Solihull, Warwickshire, dates from 1277 and was built as the chantry priest's chapel and lodging. It is in regular use for services and is known locally as the crypt chapel of All Souls. It is not known whether it originally housed the bones of the church's patron saint, but in the original stone altar there is a small area where there is an unknown relic set in lead. It is a good example of the difficulty of making distinctions between the words 'crypt' and 'undercroft'. There is very little that is cut-and-dried when it comes to exploring old churches.

Where to find crypts

Saxon crypts are very rare in parish churches today. The best known, apart from what is now Ripon Cathedral, are beneath the ancient Saxon churches at Hexham in Northumberland, Wing in Buckinghamshire, Repton in Derbyshire, and what little remains of the crypt at the Saxon church of All Saints at Brixworth, Northamptonshire. In London the City church of All Hallows by the Tower also has a Saxon crypt.

Norman/Romanesque:

London: St Mary-le-Bow
Nottinghamshire: Newark
Oxford: St Peter-in-the-East
Warwickshire: Warwick (St Mary)
West Midlands: Berkswell
Yorkshire: Lastingham

Thirteenth century:

Essex: Saffron Walden
London: St Bride, Fleet St; St Olave, Hart Street
Oxfordshire: Burford
Northumberland: Bamburgh
Sussex: Bosham
West Midlands: Coventry (St Michael)

Fourteenth century:

Bristol: St John Baptist
Dorset: Wimborne (Minster church of St Cuthburga)
Herefordshire: Madley

Bone holes – or churches where bone holes are known to have existed:

Bristol: St Mary Redcliffe, Westbury-on-Trym
Essex: Maldon (All Saints), Saffron Walden
Gloucestershire: Cirencester
Kent: Hythe
Lincolnshire: Grantham
Norfolk: Swanton Morley
Northamptonshire: Oundle, Rothwell
Oxfordshire: Witney

Easter sepulchres

These are interesting features and sometimes difficult to differentiate from tomb recesses. They are elaborate recesses, usually constructed in the Decorated period and later in the fourteenth century. They are always found on the north side of the chancel. They look like canopied tombs, which is what they were early on, without an effigy. Their purpose was to house the Blessed Sacrament, representing the body of Our Lord between Good Friday and early on Easter Day. Many Easter sepulchres were disposed of during the reign of Elizabeth I. Where they still exist some are used to this day.

An Easter sepulchre, Holy Cross parish church, Crediton, Devon.

Easter sepulchres are not as rare as you might have thought. Here are some of the churches where they can be found:

Derbyshire: Ashbourne
Devon: Bere Ferrers, Ottery St Mary, Throwleigh, West Alvington
Dorset: Tarrant Hinton
Glamorgan: Coety
Herefordshire: Ledbury
Lincolnshire: Heckington, Navenby
Norfolk: Baconsthorpe, Kelling, Northwold
Nottinghamshire: Hawton, Sibthorpe
Oxfordshire: Childrey, Sparsholt
Powys: Old Radnor
Somerset: Monksilver, Pilton, Sampford Arundel
Suffolk: Cockfield
Wiltshire: Purton
Yorkshire: Patrington

Chests and boxes

Many churches have fine old chests, which were used to store money, vestments or documents. Many have complex locks or other features of note such as interesting carving or unusual styles of ironwork. When they have survived, written parish registers, which used to be kept in them after they became obligatory in 1538, record much of the social history of Britain.

After about 1600 the chests also became the repositories of church-wardens' records and accounts, documents which often provide important information about changes associated with the Reformation and the removal of rood screens and gilden images.

Ancient parish chest, St Andrew, West Stafford, Dorset.

Among the various kinds of boxes to be found in churches are Bible boxes, many of which date from the seventeenth century and retain the original lock and hasp, collection boxes and alms (poor) boxes. After the Dissolution of the Monasteries when the relief afforded to the poor came to an abrupt end, much of the responsibility of providing aid to the poor passed to the parish churches, and in the reigns of Edward VI and Elizabeth I congregations were encouraged to help as much as possible. The old parish chest was sometimes used as an alms box, but gradually purpose-built alms boxes began to appear.

Poor box, St Peter, Great Walsingham, Norfolk.

Some fine alms boxes are to be seen at:

Devon: Pinhoe
Hampshire: Tunworth
Gloucestershire: Winchcombe
Kent: Smarden
Norfolk: Great Walsingham, Loddon
Suffolk: Parham
Wales: Dolwyddelan, Llanaber, Llaneilian
Yorkshire: Bridlington, Giggleswick, Speeton

Aumbries

These are cupboards in the north wall of the chancel where the sacred vessels and oils were kept. They are used far less for this purpose nowadays because of the fear of theft, but quite often they have been refurbished to house the Reserved Sacrament – that is, the consecrated elements 'reserved' from a celebration of the Mass or Eucharist.

Dole cupboards and dole tables

Dole cupboards and dole shelves housed bread for the poor, usually provided by a local benefactor. Most date from the Dissolution of the Monasteries or after, for the same reason as alms boxes began to appear at this time – monasteries were no longer present to feed the poor and look after passing travellers. They are usually near the entrance and may simply be open shelves, or cupboards with holes. Good examples are to be found at: All Saints, Hereford; All Saints at Milton Ernest, Bedfordshire; St Martin at Ruislip, Middlesex; St Denys at Sleaford, Lincolnshire; and St Mary's at West Chiltington, Sussex.

Early dole cupboard.

Libraries and chained books

The Church in medieval England built up very large libraries of valuable books, but these were decimated at the Reformation. Local centres of learning were not revived on the same scale, but many churches managed to build up libraries. The most famous of these is in a cathedral – at Hereford. However, several parish churches possess libraries, of which the most famous is Wimborne Minster in Dorset. A large number of churches also have one or more chained books – not only Bibles.

Chained books can be found in the following parish churches, among others:

Buckinghamshire: Broughton, Newport Pagnell
Cheshire: Backford
Cornwall: Little Petherick
Derbyshire: Dronfield
Dorset: Wimborne Minster
East Riding of Yorkshire: Bridlington
Essex: Hatfield Broad Oak
Gloucestershire: Cirencester, Fairford
Lancashire: Leyland
Lincolnshire: Grantham
Norfolk: Ranworth, Wiggenhall St Mary
Northamptonshire: Kingsthorpe, Towcester
Shropshire: Whitchurch
Somerset: Glastonbury
South Yorkshire: Hatfield
Surrey: Lingfield
Warwickshire: Wootton Wawen
Worcestershire: Bromsgrove

Odd interior markings

As well as 12 external consecration crosses (see page 40) ancient churches at their consecration would have their inside walls anointed at 12 places by the presiding bishop. Where these are still visible they are usually in the same form – a red painted cross within a circle about 8 feet from the ground – the same height as the outside.

Votive crosses and graffiti are totally different. You will occasionally see little scratchings deliberately cut into stone doorways. These are usually pilgrims' marks, otherwise known as votive crosses, indicating that the marker had committed himself (or herself) to the fulfilment of a vow – usually a visit to a well-known shrine.

Another form of graffiti to be found in old churches are masons' marks – marks cut by stonemasons to mark their work in the same way as artists sign their pictures. Masons' marks are made up of rectangles, triangles, curves, angles and intersecting lines, so when you come across them you will now be able to recognize them for what they are!

Votive crosses, masons' marks and other forms of internal graffiti may be found at the following churches:

Votive crosses
Essex: Black Notley, Castle Hedingham
Greater London: Sutton
Sussex: Westhampnett

Masons' marks
Essex: Black Notley
Gloucestershire: Tewkesbury, Winchcombe

Graffiti
Cambridgeshire: Coton
Essex: Berden, Rickling, Willingale St Christopher
Lincolnshire: Ropsley
Suffolk: Yoxford
Surrey: Compton
Sussex: Ford, Singleton, Westham

Nine Men's Morris was a game believed to have been played by clergy sitting on the stone seats in the chancel while their colleagues said offices. The markings are always the same – and sometimes found in timber stalls. The thing to look for is four squares carved in a block in the wood or stone, with each corner marked by a dot, and dots half way along each side. Intersecting lines, crossing at the middle, usually join the corners.

Maidens' garlands

These are a great oddity, worth seeking out because they are so rare – and so few people seem to have heard of them.

Otherwise known as virgins' crowns or 'crants', maidens' garlands were garlands of real or imitation flowers carried in the funeral procession of a maiden. After the funeral they were usually hung over the relevant family pew. The practice was observed in the eighteenth century. The best collections still to be seen in parish churches are at Abbotts Ann in Hampshire, Ashford-in-the-Water in Derbyshire, Minsterley in Shropshire, and St Stephens old church at Fylingdales, North Yorkshire. There is also an example at Walsham le Willows in Suffolk.

Hour glasses

After the Restoration of King Charles II in 1660 when the emphasis was placed strongly on the Word, church attendance was compulsory and sermons were expected to last at least an hour. The hour glass was intended to regulate the length to the sermon, and the sand within it usually took an hour to run through.

The hour glass was usually placed on a bracket on the wall beside the pulpit, so the preacher was able to see how long he had been preaching for. More than 100 hour glass brackets remain, but there are very few actual glasses remaining.

At Earl Stonham in Suffolk no fewer than four glasses have survived, each for a different length of time. They can also be seen at Binfield and Hurst in Berkshire, Kempsford and Shipton Solars in Gloucestershire, Pilton and Tawstock in Devon, and Compton Bassett in Wiltshire.

Organs and other musical instruments

When one thinks of music in churches one thinks automatically of organs. It is known that some forms of organ were used as far back as the tenth century, when they sometimes accompanied the singing of plainsong in monastic churches. By the end of the fifteenth century organs were common, even in small churches, and many abbey churches possessed several.

The great organ at All Hallows-by-the-Tower, London; rebuilt in 1957 and in a long line of famous organs at the church.

However, during the Reformation many were removed from churches, and in the following century the Puritans did their best to remove more. In 1644 an Act of Parliament declared that: 'All organs and the frames and the cases in which they stand in all churches and chapels shall be taken away and utterly defaced and none other hereafter set up in their place.' In this way not only the instruments but often the beautifully carved cases were destroyed. The only known pre-Reformation organ case (it houses a newer organ) is at Old Radnor in Wales. It dates from about 1525.

The restoration of Charles II in 1660 brought the return of organs, and there are several fine examples dating from the late seventeenth century in the churches of the City of London.

Organs were by no means always the only musical instruments used in churches. Throughout the eighteenth and early nineteenth centuries many churches had orchestras, the musicians often doubling their roles with those in the town band.

The musicians would play in the west galleries that began to appear in churches after the Reformation and that are still seen in many churches of the Georgian period. The town band played a leading part in church life until the middle of the nineteenth century, when they were often replaced by robed choirs of men and boys, who usually sang in the chancel. However, in country areas church orchestras often lasted a lot longer – often well into the last quarter of the nineteenth century.

Careful detective work by church explorers can sometimes reveal the evidence of this. At Parracombe old church in Devon, cut into the panelling in the cramped little west gallery is a large hole – just big enough to allow the bass fiddle player the full sweep of his bow!

As a reminder of the days when town musicians played primitive instruments, you will also, from time to time, spot ancient and obscure musical instruments in odd dusty corners or hanging on the walls of old parish churches. One of the oddest, still to be spotted occasionally, is the vamp horn or shawm. It is a type of giant megaphone into which the musician hummed and improvised harmonies. This magnified sound provided body, the idea being to assist the other instruments! The vamping horn at East Leake in Nottinghamshire is 7ft 9 in long!

On your travels round ancient churches you may find the odd long-disused example of a serpent, a low-sounding instrument with a curved long tube, a sackbut (early trombone) or pitch pipes, which were used to provide the correct note for singers.

Bells

Like the Perpendicular phase of architecture, change-ringing is one of those things that is not seen in the rest of Europe. Apart from the UK and Ireland the art of change-ringing is unknown except in countries which have had British connections.

This makes a working knowledge of bells worthwhile in its own right for any church explorers. The key things to know are that bells have been rung in churches in this country since Celtic times. It is known that they were in general use 300 years before the Norman Conquest. In medieval times the bells of parish churches marked the canonical hours and summoned the faithful to worship. They tolled the curfew and the Angelus, warned of emergencies and announced the death of a parishioner.

Like other forms of music associated with churches, bells had a bad time during the Reformation, when many rings were either silenced or removed.

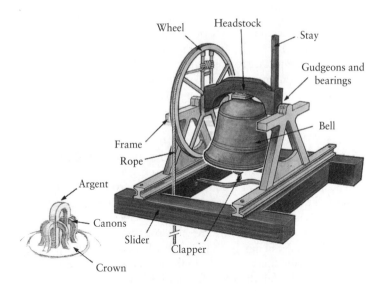

The mountings and workings of a bell.

The art of change-ringing was introduced in the mid-seventeenth century. More than 5,000 English churches have rings of five or more bells, and nearly 3,000 medieval bells are still rung in England's churches.

5

Screens, Lofts, Chantries, Roofs and Ceilings

Screens

These can vary enormously in churches old and new. Their function is to separate areas of the church while still giving an indication of what lies beyond. This means that the main screen is always at the entrance to the chancel, which is why it is known as a chancel screen or rood screen. In medieval times the screen fulfilled an important purpose because the main body of the church – the nave – was frequently used for non-religious activities.

Screens can be of timber or stone – although stone ones, especially those with vestiges of paint on them, are very rare. The Victorians often favoured wrought-iron choir screens. In contemporary churches stainless steel is more in vogue.

The first examples of wooden screens date from the 1200s and imitate the styles of the slightly earlier stone screens. However, there were, and are, several other types of screen.

Principal among these are the parclose screens. These are the screens – usually in highly carved timber but occasionally in stone – used to divide side chapels from the main body of the church.

However, by far the most fascinating are the full-sized rood screens, with their rood lofts still attached. These are very rare, and you will be very lucky if you find one where you can actually ascend, though in some instances it is possible to climb a certain distance up the spiral stairs that led up to them.

A word of historical explanation is needed here. The rood, from the Old English word meaning 'cross', is a carved image of Christ crucified (crucifix). In Saxon times carved stone roods often appeared above the doorways of churches – indeed some remain.

Parclose screen and loft, St Mary, Dennington, Suffolk.

Original complete early 16th-century rood loft, St Margaret,
St Margarets, Herefordshire.

The medieval *Great Rood* was an interior feature – a carved
and painted crucifix, erected on a beam behind the rood screen
which separated the chancel from the nave, and flanked by the
figures of the Blessed Virgin Mary and St John the Evangelist.
These figures were usually mounted on the beam.

You will see from any rood lofts you manage to discover that
these were quite substantial structures. It is known that parts of
some offices were sung from these lofts, and it is thought that in
some form or other they anticipated organ lofts, with musical
instruments being played from there.

Complete rood lofts are very rare nowadays because, together
with the great roods they supported, they were ordered to be
taken down by order of the Privy Council during the Reformation
in 1548. Again in the second half of the sixteenth century they
were frequently regarded by the Reformers as idolatrous and
destroyed. However, the screens which supported the rood lofts
were protected by legislation at the time, so many former rood
screens have survived as chancel screens.

The former presence of a rood loft explains why so often one
sees a staircase (or the remains of one) curving upwards, appar-
ently to nowhere, somewhere near the chancel arch in many old

Classical screen (early 17th century) St Peter, Walpole St Peter, Norfolk.

churches. Often there is no sign of the steps, but odd bumpy sections of stone around chancel arches provide a telltale sign. The other sure sign is when you see an odd doorway leading to nowhere positioned in the wall above you. In pre-Reformation days it almost certainly led to the rood loft above.

If the screen still has a rood on it then it is unlikely to be original. Most roods are Victorian Gothic or early twentieth-century additions.

Wooden screens

Medieval screens were generally coloured and gilded. It is possible to see traces of paint on many historical ones, especially in the West Country and East Anglia. The finest medieval examples are in Devon, where some of the best stretch from one side of the church to the other in a single unbroken line, and in East Anglia. The earliest date from the thirteenth century, though the vast majority are fourteenth or fifteenth century. The most interesting are those that retain some of their original painting.

There is a marked difference in the styles in Devon and in East Anglia. In general the Devon screens are heavier than the East Anglian screens, which tend to be lighter and more finely executed.

Fine painted medieval screen, St Helen, Ranworth, Norfolk (c.1500).

Not all wooden screens you see today are original: many were restored in the nineteenth century and the first part of the twentieth. Some are mixtures of old and new work. In the eighteenth century when many churches fell into disrepair, screens were quite frequently reduced to half height, usually as a result of wet rot caused by leaking roofs.

Fine wooden carved screens may be found in:

Buckinghamshire: Wing
Derbyshire: Kirk Langley
Devon: Ashton, Bovey Tracey, Burrington, Cullompton, Dittisham, East Portlemouth, Harborough, Marwood, Ottery St Mary, Payhembury, Rattery, Wolborough
Durham: Staindrop
Herefordshire: St Margarets
Hertfordshire: Baldock
Norfolk: Acle, Attleborough, Barton Turf, Cawston, Hunstanton, Ludham, Ranworth, South Creake, Upper Sheringham

Oxfordshire: Stanton Harcourt
Powys: Old Radnor
Somerset: Banwell, Dunster, Lapford, Minehead
Suffolk: Blythburgh, Bramfield, Dennington, Eye, Somerleyton, Westhall
Surrey: Compton, Guildford
Warwickshire: Henley-in-Arden
Wiltshire: Avebury, Compton Bassett, Hilmarton

Where to find fine screens with rood lofts:

Bedfordshire: Oakley
Berkshire: Warfield
Devon: Atherington, Marwood, Swimbridge
Herefordshire: St Margarets
Lincolnshire: Coates-by-Stow
Norfolk: Attleborough, Upper Sheringham
Northamptonshire: Ashby St Ledgers
Wiltshire: Avebury
Wales: Bettws-Newydd, Derwen, Llananno, Llanegryn, Llaneilian, Llanengan, Llanfilo Llangwm, Llangwm Uchaf, Llanrwst, Llanwnog, Montgomery, Patrishow
Yorkshire: Hubberholme, Flamborough

Later screens with lofts

A number of fine rood screens with complete roods above were built during the Gothic Revival of the nineteenth century and in the first quarter of the twentieth century.

Some of the finest are at:

Cornwall: Blisland
Dorset: Wimborne St Giles
Lincolnshire: Huttoft
Somerset: Lapford
Suffolk: Eye
Wiltshire: Mere

Stone screens

These are pretty rare but you will find them at:

Cambridgeshire: Bottisham
Derbyshire: Ilkeston, Sawley
Devon: Awliscombe, Colyton, Totnes
Dorset: Cerne Abbas
Essex: Great Bardfield, Stebbing
Gloucestershire: Berkeley
Kent: Capel le Ferne, Westwell
Lincolnshire: Tattershall
Northamptonshire: Finedon
Oxfordshire: Baulking
Somerset: Brimpton
Suffolk: Bramford

Rare early stone screen, St Nicholas, Baulking, Oxfordshire.

Chantries

A chantry was a Mass recited at an altar for the well-being of a founder or a benefactor, for the repose of his soul after death. Chantries were frequently said in small side chapels. These chantries were a popular form of endownment from the close of the thirteenth century to the Dissolution when Henry VIII abolished them in 1547.

Fifteenth-century chantry chapel, St John the Baptist, Burford, Oxfordshire.

People often left money in their wills for the saying of these Masses, believing that this process would help speed their souls through the uncomfortable state of Purgatory – a transient state (the concept was established in the twelfth century) occupied by repentant sinners who have died in grace. Not only individuals but medieval guilds endowed chantries by paying the stipends of their priests, and there were thousands of such chapels all over the country.

Chantry chapels can be small altars tucked away beside a pillar, or they can be of amazing size and splendour – virtually churches-within-a-church. One of the most famous examples of this is the Beauchamp chapel at St Mary, Warwick. Chantries like this were originally staffed by small armies of priests, some of whom lived on the church premises. Other chantry chapels are smaller affairs separated from the main body of the church by parclose screens.

Church explorers should be careful not to confuse canopied monuments with chantry chapels, which always have an altar at which Masses were celebrated.

Good examples of chantry chapels may be found in:

Berkshire: Windsor (St George's Chapel)
Buckinghamshire: Wing
Carmarthenshire: Carmarthen
Derby: Chesterfield (St Mary and All Saints), Sawley
Devon: Cullompton, Paignton, Tiverton
Dorset: Christchurch Priory
Essex: East Horndon, Halstead, Layer Marney, Writtle
Gloucestershire: Cirencester, Tewkesbury Abbey
Nottinghamshire: Newark
Oxfordshire: Burford, North Leigh
Suffolk: Dennington, Long Melford
Sussex: Boxgrove
Warwickshire: Warwick (St Mary)
Wiltshire: Bromham, Devizes
Worcestershire: Evesham (All Saints)

Roofs and ceilings

Stone roofs

One of the first things to learn here is the definition of a *vault* in a church context. The word can refer to a subterranean *burial* vault, but in this section the intention is to get you to turn your head upwards, get your binoculars out if necessary and look at the *roof* vault. An alternative – probably the best – is to lie flat on your back on the floor or on a bench. A roof vault is usually constructed of finely intersecting pieces of stone: but they can also be of timber, and even covered with plaster or even papier maché.

Fairford, Gloucestershire: the parish church of St Mary the Virgin is the only parish church in England to contain a complete set of late medieval glass. The 28 windows, the original sections of which date from the early 1500s, tell the story in pictures of the basis of the Christian faith. This window is one of the finest. It is the Great West Window, showing Christ in judgement over the world. The lower half, which shows souls being weighed in the balance, is medieval. The upper half was replaced in 1864. (Photo: J MacKechnie-Jarvis)

Sherborne Abbey, Dorset: the modern Great West Window, by John Haywood (1998). (Photo: Chris Singleton)

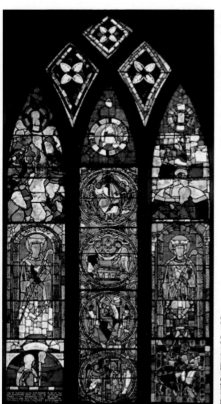

St Mary and All Saints, Rivenhall, Essex: some really beautiful late 12th and 13th-century panels in the East Window. The four circular panels in the central lancet date from 1170 and portray Christ in Majesty, a virgin and child, the Annunciation, and the entombment of the Virgin Mary. (Photo: John R Salmon)

Dorchester Abbey, Oxfordshire: the famous Tree of Jesse Window in the sanctuary dates from the early 14th century. Much of the glass is fragmentary, but it is still in its original window. The window portrays the descent of Christ from Jesse. The 'tree', with five undulating branches carved with foliage, rises from the recumbent form of Jesse, carrying figures of Old Testament prophets and kings. (Photo: Frank Blackwell)

Above: St Peter, West
Rudham, Norfolk: fine
15th-century Norwich
glass panel showing Christ
displaying his wounds.
(Photo: Lyn Stilgoe)

Right: St John Baptist,
Stanton St John,
Oxfordshire:13th-century
geometric grisaille glass in
the chancel window.

Below: St Mary the
Virgin, Waterperry,
Oxfordshire: early
(c1250–70) panels in the
chancel north window.
(Photo: Frank Blackwell)

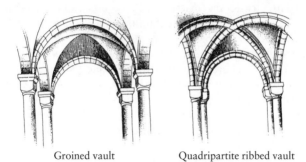

Groined vault   Quadripartite ribbed vault

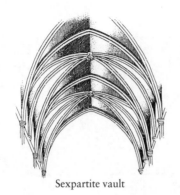

Sexpartite vault

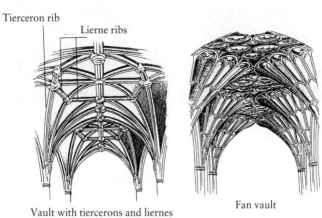

Vault with tiercerons and liernes   Fan vault

Stone vaults.

In the latter cases the material will be concealing something stronger behind, because the definition of a vault is the arched framework that supports the roof structure.

The simplest form of vaulting is the stone *barrel vault*. It is commonly found in churches of the Romanesque (Norman) period and is a simple curve supported by heavy, straight sides. A later, medieval, development of this was the similarly curved timber *wagon roof*. It is very simple and often very beautiful and is a common sight inside old parish churches in the West Country. It is invariably of timber.

Where two stone barrel vaults cross they form a *groined* or *cross* vault.

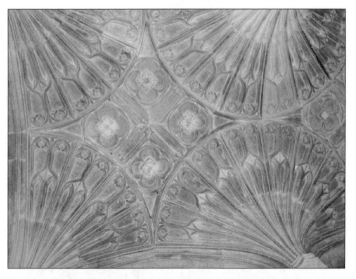

Exquisite stone fan vaulting in the ceiling of the Wilcote Chapel, St Mary, North Leigh, Oxfordshire (mid-15th century).

When the pointed arch arrived on the scene masons found that the ribs – the smaller curved members that divide the vault into compartments – multiplied. Ceilings in Early English churches were beautified by the use of *tierceron* (meaning subsidiary pairs that do not cross through the centre of the structure) vaults. In later churches of the Decorated period these were superceded by *lierne* ribs. These are ribs that cross from one boss to another, forming a star-like shape on the vault above. During the Perpendicular period ceiling ribs reached their peak of perfection with the development of fan vaulting, so-called because the trumpet shapes formed by the ceiling ribs fan out in all directions in a glorious display of the skill of the late Gothic stonemason.

Timber roofs

Fine timber roofs take many forms. When in East Anglia, be on the lookout for *angel roofs*. These glorious structures are typified by carved wooden angels, often to be seen perched on the ends of *hammer beams*. These evolved during the fifteenth century. They are shortened tie beams which project at wall-plate level and are supported from beneath by curved posts resting on stone brackets (corbels). This means of construction allows the weight of the roof to be carried across a much wider span than would previously have been possible. Hammer-beam roofs are often – indeed usually – awesome structures. They are a perfect example of how the medieval carpenter was always trying to make his roof structure more elegant, while refining its engineering so that from ground level it was quite plain what piece of work every individual piece of timber was performing.

Hammer-beam roofs are not entirely confined to the east of England. One of the finest examples in a secular setting is the roof of Westminster Hall, London.

One of the wonderful things about these great roofs of the Perpendicular period is that they were largely out of the reach of the iconoclasts, though Cromwell's men disliked them intensely, during the Protector's years in power. Sometimes, however, Puritan soldiers took shots at the angels, as can be seen very clearly if you look up at the fine angel roof in the glorious parish church of Holy Trinity, Blythburgh, Suffolk, and also the finest of all angel roofs – St Wendreda's at March, Cambridgeshire.

Tie-beam roofs are simpler than hammer-beam constructions. They are best seen in Somerset and Cheshire.

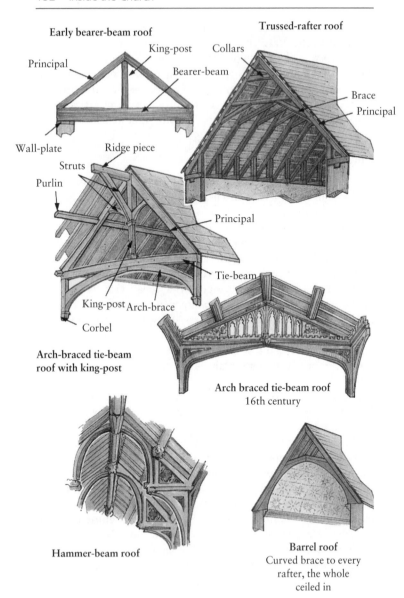

Early bearer-beam roof

King-post

Principal

Bearer-beam

Trussed-rafter roof

Collars

Brace

Principal

Wall-plate

Ridge piece

Struts

Purlin

Principal

Tie-beam

King-post   Arch-brace

Corbel

Arch-braced tie-beam roof with king-post

Arch braced tie-beam roof 16th century

Hammer-beam roof

Barrel roof Curved brace to every rafter, the whole ceiled in

Timber roofs.

Fine medieval hammer-beam roof, St Agnes, Cawston, Norfolk.
(Photo: Richard Tilbrook)

Barrel-vaulted roof with Georgian interior furnishings, St Andrew, Winterborne Tomson, Dorset.

Roof bosses

Roof bosses appear at the intersections of ribs in a vaulted roof. Their purpose is to disguise the joints of the ribs but, like wonderful timber roofs, they presented a chance for the carvers and the masons (they are found in wood and stone) to demon-

Medieval boss of green man, St Peter and St Paul, Salle, Norfolk.

Angel roof boss, St Mary, South Creake, Norfolk.

strate their skills. Roof bosses, often highly coloured, are carved with a huge variety of subjects and motifs. Heraldry looms large; so does the *green man*, an old piece of pagan mythology symbolizing fertility and the endurance of nature that was Christianized to represent the everlasting life promised by a belief in Jesus Christ. The green man appears in various guises in the structure of ancient churches up and down the country.

Again you may like to lie flat on your back to see roof bosses to best effect. Binoculars may be useful.

6

Windows, Stained Glass, Pillars and Arcades

. . . the house of the great God, which is builded with great stones, and timber is laid in the walls, and this work goeth on with diligence and prospereth in their hands
The Book of Ezra

Windows

The basic shapes and styles of windows in old churches have been explained in Part 1 (see pages 23–9).

Often the exquisite patterning of the stonework that holds the glass in a window – it is usually at the head – comes into its own inside a church because of the stained glass contained within it. The name for this is *tracery*.

Simple tracery was found in the thirteenth century. It was mainly used at the heads of lancets – the long thin main lights that usually came in groups (see pages 25–6).

Geometrical tracery arrived later in the Early English period (1200–1300). It contained far more fancy decoration at the head of the window and was a taste of the more elaborate intersecting tracery (also called Y-tracery) that emerged in the later thirteenth century. By the fourteenth century the Decorated period had arrived, so-called because window tracery and other forms of church stonework began to take on a much more flowing and waving form. This is known as *reticulated* tracery, and the ogee – a sort of elongated S-shape – predominates.

By the time the Decorated period was coming to an end in the mid-fourteenth century, this elaborate window tracery began to give way to flowing *curvilinear tracery*. The symmetrical openings of reticulated tracery lights evolved into more asymmetrical shapes.

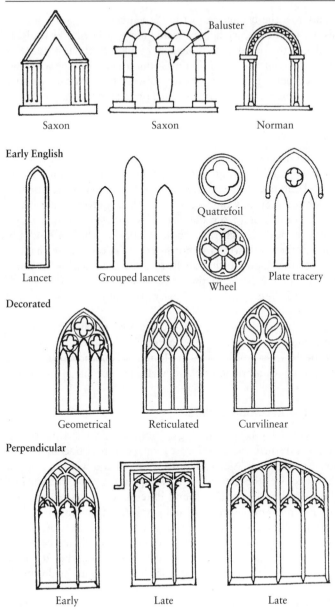

Windows.

This was the beginning of the Perpendicular period. Later in this period the tracery lights became more ordered and straight-sided – as the name 'perpendicular' implies. In the last phase of this very long period (*c*.1540) the Gothic arches over the windows flattened out dramatically and the tracery beneath became very elaborate again. It is known as *panel* or *rectilinear* tracery.

Low side windows

There is another major category of window that church explorers find fascinating. These are generally found on the south side of the chancel and used to be referred to as *leper windows* because it is thought that lepers would be left outside but given some sort of blessing or offering from the chancel via these windows. How-ever, it is now thought that these windows, which are usually found in the south-west and north-west windows of the chancel, were for the ringing of handbells to draw the attention of those working in the fields to the Mass that was being celebrated. Nowadays these features are generally referred to as *low side windows*.

Low side windows occur in every period of church building. Some, like the one at Stanton Harcourt in Oxfordshire, are very beautiful. Other notable ones are found at Faulkbourne in Essex, Rampton in Cambridgeshire and Melton Constable in Norfolk.

Stained and coloured glass

In the same way as wallpaintings, coloured pillars and arches and screens adorned the interiors of our old parish churches in medieval times, so 'glass pictures' covered the window spaces. The object was the same as in the wallpaintings – to teach people who were largely untutored and illiterate the facts about their faith in a memorable and spiritually uplifting fashion.

To the builders of our medieval churches light was highly symbolic. It was seen as directly representing God, and coloured light was the equivalent of the jewels embellishing the Heavenly City of Jerusalem. So coloured glass was inherently tied in with Christian belief.

Coloured glass is part of both the architecture and the decora-tion of a church: it is the only form of church art that is observed

St Mary, Shrewsbury: the 14th-century stained glass east window, depicting the Tree of Jesse – the lineage of Christ depicted as a tree springing from the recumbent figure of Jesse at the bottom of the window. Photo by Christopher Dalton, courtesy The Churches Conservation Trust.

Rare early 14th-century Coronation of the Virgin window, Wing, Buckinghamshire. Stained glass colour plates are to be seen between pages 148 and 149.

through refracted rather than reflected light, so its appearance can change according to the time of day and season of the year. On a bright day the light cast through stained glass windows onto walls and floors can achieve a brilliant – almost magical – quality.

However, on a bad day it can darken a church and fail to enthral, and a church with far too much heavy Victorian stained glass in the windows can appear constantly dark and sombre, and be very off-putting to visitors. This is why some church explorers find it hard to get turned on by stained glass windows.

To appreciate coloured glass you need patience – and a little basic knowledge. Not all church explorers may possess both these qualities, which is why many will hurry round an old church and pay scant attention to the glass. Then they arrive home and read the guide book or another book on churches and find they have failed to observe some ecclesiastical art of the highest quality. So this is one of those subjects it pays to learn a little about in advance of your church exploring.

* * *

For the church explorer it is useful to know the difference between very ancient medieval glass, which might date from the mid-twelfth century, and the products that resulted from the many workshops that arose during the Gothic Revival period in the nineteenth century.

The earliest church glass in England was produced by fitting pieces of coloured glass into a network of lead. The leadwork pattern was drawn out first on a large whitewashed table, and the window was built up slowly, sliding the glass pieces in. In those days glass could only be produced in small sizes, so had to be contained in a latticework of lead in order to be able to cover a window space.

You can tell the earliest glass because the surface is rather bumpy and the bubbles inside it go round in circles because the material is hand blown. Look at the reds. If they are a rich ruby colour then the glass could date from as far back as 1150. During this period, and a bit later, glaziers only had a very deep red, and to make it brighter they put a layer of white glass beneath it, so when you see ruby red glass with chips of white beneath it, it is probably medieval and not Victorian. This is called 'flashed' glass. Also in this period patterns and details were achieved by scratching away parts of the thin layer of coloured glass.

By the following century the art of *grisaille* (from the French word *gris*, meaning grey) had been invented. This was a cheaper and less laborious process – a simple form of glass painting, in which clear or white glass was painted with foliage or geometric designs.

Much grisaille glass of this period is very beautiful and contains wonderful geometric and intertwining natural forms. Because colour is only sparingly used, grisaille had the effect of increasing the amount of light coming into the building, which was previously restricted by the use of panels of deeply coloured stained glass.

By the beginning of the fourteenth century the process of *staining* glass had been discovered. This was different from the previous method of coloured glass in which various metal oxides were added to the mixture to colour the material. Instead, the glaziers painted the glass with silver nitrate ('silver staining'), then fired it in an oven. According to the number of times the glass was stained, then fired, a range of yellow tones from pale lemon to

Panel from 14th-centry window, East Harling, Norfolk.
(Photo: Richard Tilbrook)

deep orange could be produced. Unlike the earlier glass in church windows, in which each piece was a different colour, this meant that several different hues could be shown on the same piece of glass. This was an obvious advance from earlier techniques in which each piece was a different colour bound together in the network of lead. Now all the glazier had to do was paint on the different stains and draw on the outlines of the faces and heads on one piece of glass and then fire it.

You can therefore often tell glass of this period by looking at the faces of the figures. In earlier windows the figures usually have pink faces because plain white glass was not used, but once staining came in the hair is usually yellow and the faces white. The discovery of silver stain also meant that it was possible to use larger pieces of glass. The result was that less lead was used in the windows and so the light could penetrate that much easier.

Much of the finest stained glass is found in churches of the fifteenth and sixteenth centuries – the great age of church building – when large areas of the country enjoyed increasing wealth and prosperity. Rich donors would give windows just as they gave chapels and chantries and elaborate porches – nowadays we call

Fine 15th-century stained glass in the Clopton Chapel at Holy Trinity Church, Long Melford, Suffolk. The panel shows Elizabeth Talbot, Duchess of Norfolk. It is said that the artist, John Tenniel, used her as the model for his wonderful illustration of the Duchess in Alice's Adventures in Wonderland.

it sponsorship – and the new Perpendicular style permitted many windows and a feast of light.

The subjects depicted – many of the familiar biblical themes and the lives of the saints – had a far greater realism. We also see huge walls of coloured glass, with whole tiers of saints stacked one above another. It is fun to watch out for detail reflecting the medieval interpretation of saints, biblical characters wearing

Bale All Saints, Norfolk: the Annunciation of the Blessed Virgin Mary. In the detail seen here the Holy Ghost in the form of a dove comes to the Virgin. 15th-century.

contemporary British costume (especially hats!), with very medieval-looking cities in the background!

Even so, stained glass was still expensive, even for wealthy patrons, so with so many more windows in churches in this period a lot of them also incorporated a high proportion of clear glass with painting and yellow stain.

* * *

After the Reformation, with the new emphasis on the Word and the Enlightenment, the rate of stained glass production declined dramatically. One reason for this was that the figures of the saints were banned. However, it also coincided with new techniques for painting glass that were coming in from the continent, Italy in particular. The result is that we see glass windows being used far more like canvases, for the reproduction of biblical scenes. However, it was permissible to decorate windows with

Twentieth-century (1956) stained glass window commemorating the martyrdom of St Thomas à Becket, St Alphege, Solihull, West Midlands.

floral designs or heraldic shields. After the Great Fire of London in 1666 the new city churches were in the main designed to have plain glass.

Gothic architecture remained out of favour throughout the eighteenth century, so do not expect to see any spectacular stained glass windows in churches of this period. However, pictorial windows came far more into vogue, the stained glass having given way to translucent oil painting. Lead was used very rarely – usually to follow the outlines of a drawing.

During the nineteenth century stained glass in churches returned under the Victorians, but the art remained at a low ebb, with many badly designed

Bellamy memorial window, St Peter, Wolvercote, Oxford. By John Piper (1976).

and feebly drawn compositions that appear shallow and sentimental to our modern tastes. Grisaille work in particular became thin, mechanical and unimpressive.

Despite some very high quality work in the second half of the century the majority of the glass in this period was very dark and heavy in colour. The result is that the insides of some nineteenth-century churches are still very dark and, unless advanced modern lighting has been installed, it is often hard today to view all the wonderful things in the interior. Sadly one of the unfortunate legacies of the over-frequent Victorian heavy-handedness in restoring churches has been to convince some who would otherwise become church explorers that all churches are dark and gloomy inside. Fortunately, the reverse is the case.

Sometimes you can only tell whether stained glass in church windows is medieval or nineteenth-century work by consulting the church guide book. In general, however, much nineteenth-century work is much more mechanical and less spontaneous, and the colours far less subtle than the finest stained glass of the medieval period.

Towards the end of the nineteenth century, largely owing to the influence of William Morris, the art was revived using fresh ideas and images, and much good stained glass from this period can be found. The work of Sir Edward Burne-Jones in particular can be seen in a number of notable churches such as Bloxham in Oxfordshire, Cattistock in Dorset (in conjunction with William Morris), St Michael and all Angels, Waterford, Herts, and Waltham Abbey in Essex. From the second half of the twentieth century onwards church window designers have endeavoured to obscure as little light as possible and to leave bare white glass around their designs as much as they have felt able.

Millennium window, St John the Baptist, Stanton St John, Oxfordshire.

Where to see different types of stained glass

Eleventh and twelfth centuries:

Berkshire: Aldermaston,
Derbyshire: Dalbury
Essex: Rivenhall
Herefordshire: Ledbury, Madley
Kent: Brabourne
Oxfordshire: Dorchester Abbey
Sussex: Mitchelham Priory
Wiltshire: Wilton

Thirteenth century:

Buckinghamshire: Chetwode
Derbyshire: Ashbourne
Durham: Lanchester
Essex: White Notley
Gloucestershire: Bibury
Herefordshire: Madley
Leicestershire: Twycross
Norfolk: South Acre
Oxfordshire: Stanton St John, Waterperry
Surrey: West Horsley
Warwickshire: Rowington
Wiltshire: Wilton
Yorkshire: Normanton

Fourteenth century:

Bedfordshire: Cockayne Hatley
Buckinghamshire: Chetwode, Hitcham
Cumbria: Bowness-on-Windermere, Cartmel
Devon: Bere Ferrers
Durham: Wycliffe
Essex: Hatfield Peverel
Gloucestershire: Cirencester, Deerhurst, Tewkesbury Abbey
Herefordshire: Eaton Bishop, Madley
Kent: Boughton Aluph, Selling

Lincolnshire: Carlton Scroop, Heydour, Wrangle
Norfolk: Bale, Bawburgh, Elsing, Pulham St Mary
Northamptonshire: Lowick, Stanford on Avon
Northumberland: Morpeth
Nottinghamshire: Fledborough, Halam, Newark
Oxfordshire: Asthall, Dorchester Abbey
Somerset: Compton Bishop
Staffordshire: Checkley, Church Leigh, Enville
Surrey: Chiddingfold
Sussex: Cowfold, Hooe, Winchelsea
Worcestershire: Bredon, Fladbury, Kempsey, Mamble
Yorkshire: Acaster Malbis, Dewsbury, York (St Denys, Walmgate,
   St Martin-cum-Gregory, St Michael-le-Belfrey)

Fifteenth and sixteenth centuries:

Bristol: (St Mary Redcliffe)
Buckinghamshire: Drayton Beauchamp, Hillesden
Cambridgeshire: Burghley
Cheshire: Malpas
Cornwall: Golant, St Kew, St Neot
Cumbria: Greystoke
Derbyshire: Norbury
Devon: Doddiscombsleigh, Torbryan
Dorset: Bradford Peverell, Melbury Bubb
Essex: Abbess Roding, Margaretting
Gloucestershire: Bledington, Buckland, Fairford, North Cerney,
   Rendcomb
Herefordshire: Abbey Dore, Llanwarne, Ross-on-Wye,
   Weobley
Hertfordshire: South Mimms
Kent: Elham, Patrixbourne
Leicestershire: Launde
Lincolnshire: Stamford (St John Baptist), Tattershall, Wrangle
Norfolk: East Harling, Hingham, Norwich (St Peter Hungate,
   St Peter Mancroft), Salle, Wiggenhall, Wighton
Northamptonshire: Stanford on Avon
Oxfordshire: Brightwell Baldwin, Burford, Shiplake
Shropshire: Ludlow, Shrewsbury (St Mary)

Somerset: Glastonbury (St John), Langport, Mark, Nettlecombe, Orchardleigh
Staffordshire: Hamstall Ridware
Suffolk: Combs, Gipping, Long Melford
Sussex: Ticehurst
Warwickshire: Merevale, Warwick (St Mary)
Worcestershire: Great Malvern Priory
Yorkshire: Selby Abbey, Thornhill, York (All Saints, North Street; All Saints, Pavement; St Helen; St Michael, Spurriergate)

Seventeenth and eighteenth centuries:

Bedfordshire: Northill
Buckinghamshire: Addington, Stoke Poges
Cambridgeshire: Wimpole
Essex: Lambourne
Herefordshire: Abbey Dore, Shobdon
London: City (St Andrew Undershaft; St Botolph)
Manchester: St Ann
Northamptonshire: Apethorpe
Shropshire: Shrewsbury (St Alkmund)
Tyne & Wear: Newcastle upon Tyne (St John Baptist)
Worcestershire: Great Witley
Yorkshire: Acomb, York (St Martin-cum-Gregory)

Nineteenth century:

Buckinghamshire: Ellesborough
Cambridgeshire: Godmanchester, Prickwillow
Cheshire: Marple
Cumbria: Ambleside, Troutbeck
Derbyshire: Youlgreave
Devon: Ottery St Mary
Dorset: Cattistock
Essex: Great Waltham
Greater Manchester: Pendlebury
Hertfordshire: Waterford
Huntingdon district: Little Gidding, Ramsey
Lincolnshire: Crowland Abbey

London: Wandsworth (All Saints)
Norfolk: Sculthorpe
Northamptonshire: Middleton Cheney
Northumberland: Alnwick
Oxfordshire: Bloxham, Dorchester Abbey
Staffordshire: Hoar Cross
Suffolk: Lowestoft (St Margaret; St Matthew)
Sussex: Brighton (St Michael), Selsey
Worcestershire: Hanley Castle, Rochford, Worcester (St Martin)
Yorkshire: Nun Monkton, Tadcaster, Scarborough (St Martin)

Twentieth century:

Berkshire: Farnborough
Cambridgeshire: Babraham
Cheshire: Marple
Cumbria: Lanercost Priory
Devon: Dean Prior, Doddiscombsleigh, Exmouth, Plymouth (St Andrew)
Dorset: Cattistock, Sturminster Newton
Essex: Great Canfield
Hampshire: Boldre, Selborne
Herefordshire: Brockhampton
Kent: Tudeley
London: Blackfriars (Christ Church), Bromley (St Mary), Pinner, Westminster (St Margaret), Wimbledon (St Mary)
Norfolk: Norwich (St Peter Mancroft)
Northamptonshire: Wellingborough (St Mary)
Nottinghamshire: Misterton
Oxfordshire: Dorchester, Wolvercote
Somerset: Nettlecombe
Suffolk: Aldeburgh, Leiston, Snape
Sussex: Eastbourne (St Mary), Rye, Winchelsea
Tyne & Wear: Wallsend
Wiltshire: Chippenham, Cricklade (St Sampson)

Pillars and arcades

People get confused by these terms, so here are a few definitions:

A *pillar* is a free-standing vertical structure of stone or wood which acts as a support. In a church it frequently supports an *arcade,* which is a series of arches, usually open and often very elegant, that divide up sections of a church. An *arch* is a curved structure above and between the pillars. The style of the arches usually provides a good clue as to the architectural period of the church. The difference between a pillar and a column is that, while both are upright, a column usually has both a *base* and a *capital.* The base is naturally broad and solid, but again the style will give you a clue as to its age.

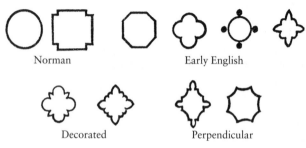

Norman   Early English

Decorated   Perpendicular

Column cross-sections.

The capital is the head, shaped like an inverted bell. Its function is to provide an area to support the masonry above that is larger than the supporting column beneath.

Arcades are one of the most attractive elements of old parish churches. A really lovely arcade, with either round or pointed arches, will hit you as a feature when you step inside the church. Arcades usually form the divide between the nave and its aisles. An aisle is usually an extension of the nave to the side, the arcade being the structure that divides the two. Arcades are tremendously important to the church explorer, who is primarily interested in how the fabric of churches developed. This is because they were very often added to the building as the church and the community became more prosperous. Conversely, when churches have shrunk in size there might be an indication of where a long-vanished arcade and aisle used to stand.

Fine arcade of pillars in the Decorated style, St Peter and St Paul, Carbrooke, Norfolk. (Photo: Richard Tilbrook)

The sumptuous nave of St Thomas, Salisbury, where the delicate Perpendicular pillars form a carefully sculpted arcade which is lit by light pouring in from the large 16th-century windows.

Perhaps the most important arch of all is the *chancel arch*. This is the arched opening in the eastern wall of the nave that gives access to the chancel. It occurs in most ancient churches and often houses the chancel screen (see page 140). The style of the chancel arch often gives you a clue as to the age of the chancel. If it was inserted later than the nave, for example in the Perpendicular period, then it will probably have a very shallow point to it and lead to a chancel built in the Perpendicular style, indicating that it was probably rebuilt on the site of an earlier chancel. To the side of the chancel arch on either side there may be a squint, or hagioscope. This is a deep hole cut obliquely through the wall in order to provide a view of the main altar from a subsidiary altar. These devices were provided so that a chantry priest (see page 147) could synchronize his celebration of the Mass with that at the High Altar. If you are a regular church explorer you will probably have seen several examples of these features, which are quite common but differ enormously from church to church.

7

Wallpaintings, Monuments and Other Internal Features

And then I know the mist is drawn
A lucid veil from coast to coast
And in the dark church like a ghost
The tablet glimmers to the dawn
Tennyson

Wallpaintings

Churches must have looked altogether different when virtually all their internal surfaces, including a great deal of the stonework, were covered with wallpaintings. It must have been a riot of colour – like a large picturebook of painted plaster.

You certainly have to use your imagination to build up a mental picture of what the interiors of these churches must have been like, because most of the wallpaintings are now fragmentary. However, there is plenty of scope for you to try, because around 2,000 churches in the UK contain traces of ancient wallpaintings. These range from very distinct and famous sets, like the early frescoes at Kempley in Gloucestershire or Coombes in West Sussex, or the great Dooms, such as the one at Oddington in Gloucestershire, to tiny fragments.

Scholars today believe that from the early thirteenth century onwards it is safe to assume that virtually all churches would have been painted throughout. The aim of wallpaintings, in an age in which few were literate, was to teach. After all, up to the end of the fifteenth century there were no printed books. Service books, sacred literature – even whole Bibles – had to be laboriously copied by hand. We believe wallpaintings were also intended to draw people into their faith, so art historians usually refer to them as 'devotional art'.

Church wallpaintings often contain terrifying images warning of the fate of those who misbehave. This wallpainting at the parish church of St Michael and St Mary, Melbourne, Derbyshire, is generally interpreted to be a warning against the evils of gossip.

To many church explorers wallpaintings, although not as rare as people often seem to think, give an added dimension when visiting a church. With the aid of the guidebook – it is to be hoped there is one – it is always fun to try and work out what the paintings are attempting to portray and what they must have looked like in their heyday. You must stand well back to appreciate them. Old church wallpaintings usually depict not only the lives of the saints and scenes from the Scriptures, but also terrifying images of the inevitability of death and of divine judgement and retribution.

Experienced church explorers will know only too well that nearly all these wallpaintings are incomplete, because they were whitewashed over and replaced with biblical texts by the Reformers in the sixteenth and seventeenth centuries. This is the reason why, in the majority of churches where they can be seen, only small fragments of wallpaintings are left. However, it is also very stimulating and great fun trying to pick out main themes.

Somehow wallpaintings are a graphic means of giving us a sense of the great age of these old churches, which are often the only ancient buildings in their community widely open to the public. Because of the primitive way they were executed – it is believed by itinerant workmen or artists – we can see here the work of local grassroots people, rather than of the educated classes that to all intents and purposes ran the Church as an institution.

It is possible to identify some of the popular recurring figures with comparative ease. By far the most common of these is St Christopher, and you will usually find him near the entrance of the church. He appeared a great deal because people liked to travel under the patronage of this great saint, who performed the role of a kind of holy minister of transport. When his image appears it is usually opposite the south door of the church and it is thought that pilgrims passing by would see him, pop in, and say a prayer. In an age in which the prospect of death was never far away, some believed that by looking at his image death could be delayed by a day. The huge figure usually has a staff and a long beard and is carrying the Christ child on his shoulder across a river full of fish and other assorted figures.

You might find the small book, *Medieval Wall Paintings*, by E. Clive Rouse, of interest (see Bibliography). As well as including a gazeteer of churches where wallpaintings are to be found

Wallpaintings in ancient churches often have such faint outlines that it takes a keen eye to spot them. The two images shown here are, nonetheless, fairly common ones. They are St George on his charger slaying the dragon and St Christopher with his staff and the Christ Child on his shoulder. The St George is at St Nicholas, Baulking, Oxfordshire, and the St Christopher at St Peter and St Paul, Pickering, North Yorkshire.

*Look out for painted pillars. It is safe to assume
that in our ancient parish churches every surface
that could take paint was indeed painted.*

throughout England there is lots of other useful information, including how the wonderful earthy pigments – browns and yellows and oranges – were obtained and prepared.

Popular recurring themes in wallpaintings

These include Bible stories from the Old and New Testaments; lives of the saints; single figures of saints, apostles and martyrs; moral or didactic themes, and purely decorative schemes.

The last were often applied directly onto stone: it was felt necessary to decorate even fine stone surfaces on unplastered features such as arches and pillars. Traces can still be seen today in many ancient churches. The most common scheme of this sort was the masonry pattern, or imitation stone joint, often painted

Two recurring images found in Doom paintings in many ancient churches are the Jaws of Hell (left) with the damned being drawn inside, and hairy-horned demons (right), seemingly taking pleasure in their wickedness.

on the plaster that covered rubblestone walls, especially in chancels.

The most common moral or didactic theme was the Last Judgement. These are more commonly known as 'Doom paintings', and were usually positioned over the chancel arch, often painted on a board. The idea seems to have been to warn the congregation of the horrible fate that awaited those who did not lead exemplary lives on earth.

The usual arrangement was the figure of Christ Triumphant, showing his wounds and seated on a rainbow in judgement, with heaven on one side and hell on the other, and sometimes St Michael with scales. The dead rise from their graves. The heavenly mansions usually look uncomfortable, but the artist really enjoyed himself much more on the other side – hell. Here are usually the jaws of a large dragon (although as it is usually described as a 'hell mouth' we can assume the device originated with the story of Jonah and the whale) with huge teeth and all enveloped in bright red flames. Horrible looking demons with red-hot chains and pitchforks secure as many customers as possible!

St Michael and All Angels, Copford, Essex: this church has one of the most important collections of ecclesiastical wallpaintings in the country. The earliest date from the mid 12th century, the latest from the 1880s.

St Lawrence, Broughton, Buckinghamshire: a general view of the interior of this church, famous for its wallpaintings, which date from the 14th and 15th centuries. (Photo courtesy The Churches Conservation Trust)

Above and below left: two details from the 15th-century Doom, or Last Judgement, painting at St Peter's, Wenhaston, Suffolk. They are set on a wooden panel.
Below right: Ashby St Ledgers, Northamptonshire: a gruesome-looking skeleton holding a spade in one hand and a pick-axe in the other. Believed to be 16th century. It is overpainted on top of earlier frescoes.

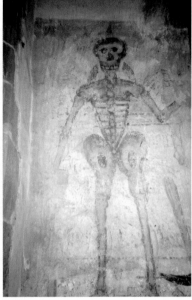

Left: St James, Cameley, Somerset: some of the fine wallpaintings in this church, which is in the care of the Churches Conservation Trust. These are fragments of the Ten Commandments, painted over the chancel arch. They date from the early 17th century. (Photo courtesy The Churches Conservation Trust).

Below left: St Thomas, East Shefford, Berkshire: two wallpaintings from different ages over the chancel arch. The paintings above probably date from the 15th century. The badly damaged painting below dates from about 1100 and is very early for a wallpainting in England. (Photo courtesy The Churches Conservation Trust)

Below right: St Faith, Little Witchingham, Norfolk: the comprehensive wallpaintings in this church include these elaborate vinescroll motifs on the nave arcade. They are believed to date from the second quarter of the 14th century. (Photo courtesy The Churches Conservation Trust)

St. Peter, Stourton, Wiltshire: an attractive wall plaque dating from 1724.

St Mary, Dennington, Suffolk: the magnificent alabaster effigies of Sir William Phelip (Lord Bardolph), who fought with Henry V at Agincourt and his wife, the Lady Joan (1441).

Two elaborate 18th-century wall monuments. Above left: 18th-century splendour in the church of St Mary Magdalene, Sherborne, Gloucestershire: a monument signed and dated 1791, in which a life-sized angel holding a medallion of the deceased and his wife tramples underfoot a skeleton representing Death. Above right: monument to Margaret, Marchioness of Caernarvon, Avington, Hampshire, who had the church built in 1768.

Wallpaintings may be seen in the following churches:

Masonry patterns and other decorative schemes
Buckinghamshire: Bledlow, Haddenham, Padbury, Weston
    Turville
Dorset: Wareham (St Martin)
Gloucestershire: Duntisbourne Rouse, Stoke Orchard
Hampshire: East Wellow
Sussex: Clayton, Plumpton

Figures of the saints
Bedfordshire: Chalgrave
Berkshire: Aldermaston
Buckinghamshire: Broughton, Little Kimble
Cheshire: Mobberley
Cornwall: Breage, Poughill, St Just-in-Penwith, St Keverne
Devon: Axmouth, Sidbury
Dorset: Cerne Abbas, Tarrant Crawford
Essex: Fairstead, Great Canfield
Gloucestershire: Baunton, Hailes, Kempley
Greater London: Hayes
Hampshire: Idsworth, Winchester (St John)
Isle of Wight: Shorwell
Lincolnshire: Corby Glen
Norfolk: Cawston, Fritton, Haddiscoe, Paston, Hemblington
Northamptonshire: Ashby St Ledgers, Castor, Croughton
Oxfordshire: Bloxham, South Newington
Somerset: Wedmore
Suffolk: Bardwell
Sussex: Wisborough Green
Wiltshire: Great Chatfield, Lydiard Tregoze, Oaksey
Worcestershire: Wickhamford

Bible stories
Buckinghamshire: Bledlow, Chalfont St Giles
Clwyd: Llangar
Cornwall: Breage
Derbyshire: Dale
Devon: Axmouth, Sidbury

Dorset: Cranbourne, Gussage St Andrew
Essex: Copford, Fairstead, Great Burstead
Gloucestershire: Kempley
Kent: Barfreston Brook, Cliffe, West Kingsdown
Leicestershire: Lutterworth
Norfolk: Attleborough, Little Melton
North Yorkshire: Easby, Pickering
Northamptonshire: Croughton
Oxfordshire: Chalgrove, North Stoke, South Newington,
   Swalcliffe
Rutland: Lyddington
Shropshire: Edstaston
Somerset: Sutton Bingham
South Glamorgan: Llantwit Major
Suffolk: Hoxne
Surrey: West Horsley, Witley
Sussex: Clayton, Coombes, Trotton, West Chiltington
Warwickshire: Wootton Wawen
Wiltshire: Purton
Worcestershire: Martley

Dooms
There are about 70 surviving, many fragmentary. Here are some
of the best:

Berkshire: Ashampstead
Bedfordshire: Wymington
Buckinghamshire: Broughton, Little Missenden, Penn
Cambridgeshire: Chesterton, Great Shelford
Gloucestershire: Oddington, Stowell
Lincolnshire: Corby Glen
Oxfordshire: Combe, Hornton, North Leigh, South Leigh
Suffolk: Stanningfield, Wenhaston
Surrey: Chaldon (ladder of salvation)
Sussex: Clayton, Patcham, Trotton
Wiltshire: Dauntsey, Salisbury (St Thomas)

Wallpaintings: methods and dating

There are very few examples left in England from the Norman or Romanesque period. The best-known are the frescoes at the old church at Kempley, Gloucestershire. They have been dated to the early twelfth century or perhaps even earlier. Unlike most of the church wallpaintings in this country they were painted on wet plaster, so technically they are *frescoes* in which, we presume, the artist and plasterer worked together. The well-known examples of ancient church wallpaintings carried out using this technique are in the so-called West Sussex group of Hardham, Clayton and Coombes, where the techniques used were similar to those used at Kempley. These early wallpaintings are characterized by their primitive pigments – just black and white, red and yellow, although amazing effects were produced from them.

The method used in most medieval English churches is the *secco* technique. In other words, the wall was completely plastered and dry (or nearly dry) when the colouring was applied.

Monuments

You may not believe it, but church monuments can be great fun! Herein lies the world of swagger and sentiment, sumptuous painting and modelling. At the other end of the spectrum lie pathos and genuine humility.

For the most amusing 'rustic' monuments look at some of the small country churches like Bramfield in Suffolk.

Here a simple floor inscription rather crudely carved tells us about Bridgett Applewhaite who died in 1737 'after the Fatigues of a Married Life . . . born (*sic*) by her with Incredible Patience . . .' having decided four years later 'to run the Risk of a Second Marriage-Bed' only to die ('DEATH forbad the Banns') suddenly when she fell to the ground 'In Terrible Convulsions Plaintive Groans . . . without Recovery of her Speech or Senses'.

For the most grandiose monuments, look to the eighteenth century. At the Baroque church of St Michael at Great Witley in Worcestershire it is said that the cost of the enormous monument to the first Lord Foley – reputedly the tallest such monument in England – was £2,000, a vast sum indeed in 1735 when it was completed.

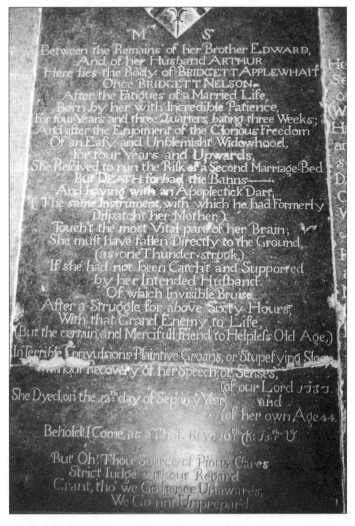

M
S

Between the Remains of her Brother EDWARD,
And of her Husband ARTHUR
Here lies the Body of BRIDGETT APPLEWHAIT
Once BRIDGETT NELSON.
After the Fatigues of a Married Life,
Born by her with Incredible Patience,
For four Years and three Quarters, bating three Weeks;
And after the Enjoiment of the Glorious Freedom
Of an Easy, and Unblemisht Widowhood,
For four Years, and Upwards,
She Resolved to run the Risk of a Second Marriage-Bed,
But DEATH forbad the Banns——.
And having with an Apoplectick Dart,
(The same Instrument, with which he had Formerly
Dispatcht her Mother,)
Toucht the most Vital part of her Brain;
She must have fallen Directly to the Ground,
(as one Thunder-strook,)
If she had not been Catcht and Supported
by her Intended Husband
Of which Invisible Bruise,
After a Struggle for above Sixty Hours,
With that Grand Enemy to Life,
(But the certain and Mercifull Friend to Helpless Old Age,)
In Terrible Convulsions Plaintive Groans, or Stupefying Sleep,
without Recovery of her Speech, or Senses,
She Dyed, on the 12th day of Sep in ÿ Year ⎰ of our Lord 1737.
⎱ and
⎰ of her own Age 44.

Behold! I Come, as a Theif. Rev. 16th Ch: 15th. V

But Oh! Thou Source of Pious Cares
Strict Iudge without Regard
Grant, tho' we Go hence Unawares,
We Go not Unprepard.

*Eighteenth-century floor tablet to Bridgett Applewhaite,
Bramfield, Suffolk.*

Eighteenth-century memorial to Sir John Dutton in full Roman attire, very much of its time, St Mary Magdalene, Sherborne, Gloucestershire.

The serious point is that church explorers need to be able to 'read monuments' if they are to get the most out of them, appreciate the funny bits, and also learn all the interesting things they tell us about how society was organized at the time.

First, remember that you had to be a person of status (or wish to be remembered as such!) to have a monument erected in a church, so churches with splendid collections of monuments are usually, but not always, churches that have long associations with families of high social status. Look therefore towards churches that were built by the owners of grand houses.

These grand monuments tell us not only about subjects such as costume, heraldry and family and national history, but also about styles in art – sculpture in particular. Many of them are very strong on technique and exceptionally well executed. We know that in the seventeenth century specialist teams of modellers, sculptors and metalworkers came over from Italy and the Low Countries to create flamboyant, often hugely expensive, monuments to local grandees.

However, just as it is thought that teams of stonemasons were often responsible for the carving inside and outside of churches in the same area, so it is believed that teams of memorial artists moved around, working on different churches. Specialists on church monuments make it their business to note the intricacies of a particular style and see if they can spot the same techniques and stylistic traits in other monuments in the same part of the country.

If you become really interested in the finer points of monuments there is a Church Monuments Society. They have a useful website: www.churchmonumentssociety.org. Perhaps heraldry is a particular interest of yours.

Because of their long history, old churches in England in particular are very rich in monuments. They vary in size from small, perfectly formed head-on-shoulders busts in high relief mounted on stone shelves on chancel walls to huge multi-coloured effigies of the deceased at prayer in full Elizabethan formal attire mounted on grand pedestals in prominent positions in the nave.

The main reason for these splendid monuments to the rich and the great is that in England in particular we have had so many powerful landed families. Successive monarchs in the medieval period relied on these barons for support of both the physical and material variety. Many of the finest monuments, therefore, tell you a great deal about politics. This is well illustrated when you have enduring sets of monuments to the same dynasty. Excellent examples of this can be found in some of the great churches of the Perpendicular period such as St Michael, Framlingham, Suffolk, and Stoke-by-Nayland in the same county. In the case of the former you can see the elaborate tomb chests of three generations of the Howards, dukes of Norfolk, who during the religious upheavals of the sixteenth century managed to fall both in and out of favour with both Henry VIII and Elizabeth I.

At Stoke-by-Nayland there are monuments to earlier generations of the same families, and a plaque in the east end of the south aisle demonstrates how some members of local families became unwittingly embroiled in the great struggle between the houses of York and Lancaster at the end of the fourteenth century that culminated in the Wars of the Roses.

Countless tomb chests and other fine monuments in churches throughout the country tell a similar tale of political and religious rivalries and intrigue in the turbulent times of the sixteenth and seventeenth centuries.

St John the Baptist, Burford, Oxfordshire: tomb to Sir Lawrence Tanfield, erected by his wife in 1628.

How monuments evolved

In the twelfth and thirteenth centuries the stone coffins of people of status were usually covered by a stone slab, often incised with a cross, and possibly some symbols of the person's rank or occupation – for example, a sword and shield for a knight, or a bell or a fish for tradesmen of varying kinds. So don't forget to look down as well as up when touring an ancient church.

In these early days when only priests and people of rank or status were buried in churches, even then the actual grave may well have been outside in the churchyard rather than beneath the

Alabaster effigies of Sir William Wilcote and his wife, Wilcote chantry chapel, St Mary, North Leigh, Oxfordshire. Early fifteenth century.

floor of the church. All too often we just do not know the exact site of the burial.

Understandably things moved on. By the mid-thirteenth century the tomb chest had made its entry. Anyone visiting an old church will be familiar with these. They look rather like stone altars and are often painted and gilded and frequently have effigies of the deceased on top of them. Although many of these are extremely beautiful they can also be quite bizarre. Great and lesser dignitaries may be depicted on their tombs as pious, proud, reverent, self-assertive or humble. We know that quite often these effigies were commissioned before the death of the person to be commemorated, so they were clearly a form of self-glorification.

It is often possible to date the effigies from the postures adopted. Early effigies usually showed the deceased alive and standing, even though their physical posture on the slab was recumbent. In the thirteenth century the strictly recumbent position began to take over, the figure lying on its back with clothing draped over the slab. At first the figures were very rigid, but by about 1350 the recumbent posture, with legs straight and hands together in prayer, began to appear. Similar effigies in wood are

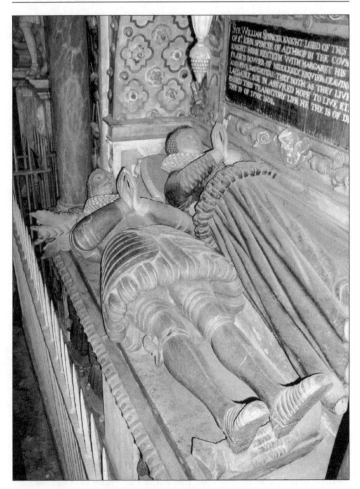

St Bartholomew, Yarnton, Oxfordshire: Sir William Spencer and his wife (1609).

still to be found (though rare). There are still traces of colour to be found on some of these effigies, leading experts to believe that, like so many elements in a church in medieval times, they were originally painted all over.

Section of a 16th-century memorial to William Lenthall and his wife, Jane, St Mary, North Leigh, Oxfordshire.

By the fourteenth century tombs like these were often canopied and set in recesses in the wall although many remained free-standing. As the fifteenth century approached the job of the master mason was taken over by the specialist creator of tombs and monuments. We know that alabaster workshops existed, especially in the north Midlands, where it was mined. The other common material used in the finest monuments was marble.

Effigies gradually became less stiff, and by the fifteenth century they had often adopted more lifelike recumbent poses. This period – the 1400s and 1500s – was also the time when the sides of tombs were often decorated with 'weepers' – small figures of members of the person's family – or of saints and angels. This was also the time when tombs were often decorated with elaborately vaulted canopies, sometimes resplendent with pinnacles, and there was also a great deal of heraldic decoration.

At about the same time the cultural winds blowing in from Europe brought with them the unmistakable signs of what we call the Renaissance. Tombs started to include Classical features such as angular pediments – rather akin to the gables of houses – running over the top. Elaborate tombs of this sort dating from before the Civil War were often damaged by Cromwell's men in the mid-seventeenth century. Later in the seventeenth century wall-mounted monuments showing only the head and shoulders, usually mounted in a circular or oval frame, began to appear.

This was the age of the Baroque, a very exhuberant style characterized by expansive curvaceous forms, in which the

Altar-style tomb chest to Sir James Phelyppe, Bart., who died in 1652, Church of St Mary and St Michael, Stoke Charity, Hampshire.

inscriptions were as over-elaborate as the monuments themselves. This style lasted well into the eighteenth century, and a popular memorial form at the time was the 'medallion portrait'. This was a wall-mounted effigy, its simplest form being a profile of the head alone in low relief. Eighteenth-century effigies are characterized by the textures and styles of clothes and wigs that were fashionable at the time, being meticulously observed – usually in marble. Figures are often shown sitting or standing in languid, often theatrical, poses, frequently dressed in Classical costume harking back to the days of ancient Greece and Rome, the men often depicted as Roman heroes. The monuments in this age are often stupendous in size and execution, and the epigraphs pompous and verbose. It all smacks of self-glorification rather than Christian humility.

Cartouche tablets are a type of wall monument common in the seventeenth and eighteenth centuries that are designed to look like sheets of paper with the sides rolled up. They are usually of marble.

In the nineteenth century monuments continued to be Classical in the first part of the century, which was the time of the Greek Revival. The most conspicuous indication of this was the imitation of ancient Greek *stele* monuments. Stele is a decorative motif consisting of a rectangular slab surmounted by a low triangular pediment and carved on its face with figures or other devices in low or high relief. The style was heavily influenced by

Early 20th-century grandeur: bronze memorial to the 3rd Marquess of Salisbury, Queen Victoria's Prime Minister (1903), Parish church of St Etheldreda, Hatfield, Hertfordshire.

the Elgin Marbles, then newly arrived in England. The style was more sentimental than the rigid poses adopted in the eighteenth century.

In nineteenth-century church monuments there were far more overtones of the 'religious' than was evident in the previous century, for most of which the Church of England was at a low ebb. White marble was the material invariably used for this type of monument. However, as the century progressed the taste for Gothic Revival made itself felt. Gothic decoration again became fashionable, as did Gothic canopies over tombs. At the end of the nineteenth century new styles such as the Art Nouveau were beginning to emerge.

By the end of Victoria's reign the erection of large-scale monuments began to decline. Taste began to change, and as the twentieth century progressed the creation of monuments declined dramatically. Today new large monuments inside churches are extremely rare.

Materials

Alabaster, a form of gypsum mined in Nottinghamshire and Derbyshire, was traditionally the prime material for the construction of elaborate monuments. It was widely used for effigies because of the speed and ease with which it could be carved. When finely finished and painted, alabaster is exceptionally smooth to the touch. The use of alabaster declined in the eighteenth and early nineteenth centuries in favour of marble but was revived in Victorian times, although then monuments were rarely painted, as they usually were in medieval times. Purbeck marble from Dorset was also widely used for monuments in the early medieval period, while occasionally wood and bronze were used. On the later family tombs brass, copper and even enamel and cast iron were used.

Gruesome effigies – otherwise known as sepulchral monuments

In many church monuments of the fifteenth to seventeenth centuries there is a representation of the dead person as a cadaver – often in quite a gruesome fashion – perhaps as a decaying corpse, even with worms at work, or certainly in an advanced state of decay. The idea was to remind the living of the decay of the body, and so to prompt them to seek salvation. Sometimes the effigy is on the top layer, clad in respondent robes of high office, while beneath is a skeleton or shrouded body. Sometimes it comes in the form of a brass – see the section on brasses (pages 201–9). This is again an intriguing area of study for many fascinated by church monuments.

This practice appears to have been borrowed from continental Europe and is thought to have originally been associated with the court of the pious King Henry VI (1422–61). The general thinking behind these effigies (in an age in which death was much closer to home than it is today) seems to have been a reminder that death, in the Christian view, is but a passing phase and the body counts as nothing.

Examples are to be found at:

Cheshire: Acton, Bunbury, Chester (St John)
Cumbria: Lowther
Devon: Feniton
Gloucestershire: Sherbourne
Hertfordshire: Hatfield
Norfolk: Stratton Strawless
Northamptonshire: King's Sutton
Nottinghamshire: Holme
Oxfordshire: Fyfield
Suffolk: Bury St Edmunds (St Mary), Lowestoft, Yoxford
Surrey: Egham, Guildford (Holy Trinity)
Yorkshire: Burton Agnes

Tomb of Dame Elizabeth Brockett and her mother, Dame Agnes Sanders (early 17th century), Parish church of St Etheldreda, Hatfield, Hertfordshire.

Heart burials

Occasionally you will see a small niche, often in the chancel or sanctuary of a church, and inside it what looks like a medallion, containing the head and shoulders of a figure with two hands grasping an extra large heart.

Heart burial of a crusader's heart, St Giles, Coberley, Gloucestershire.

These are heart burials, and are something of a mystery. They are often thought to date from the time of the Crusades. When a soldier died on the battlefield overseas it was obviously difficult to convey his body home, so it was usually laid to rest in foreign soil. However, if the dead man had willed that his heart should be returned to his own village church for burial, this request was often carried out.

Not a great many heart burials survive and some of them are very hard to confirm as definitive heart burials. As many of the images are unidentified it is also hard to tell whether the knight whose effigy is portrayed was a crusader or not.

Heart burials can be seen at:

Dorset: Mappowder, Stinsford
Gloucestershire: Coberley
Herefordshire: Castle Frome
Huntingdon district: Yaxley
Kent: Brabourne
Oxfordshire: Hatford
Shropshire: Burford
Sussex: Horsted Keynes
West Midlands: Halesowen Abbey
Worcestershire: Bredon

Other fine monuments

There are excellent examples in churches in many counties.

Here are a few suggestions:

Bedfordshire: Bromham, Cardington, Dunstable, Flitton, Old
   Warden, Sutton, Tilsworth, Toddington, Turvey, Willington
Berkshire: Aldworth, Bisham, Chaddleworth, East Shefford,
   Shottesbrooke, Sonning
Buckinghamshire: Amersham, Chenies, Clifton Reynes,
   Edlesborough, Gayhurst, Lillingstone Dayrell, Quainton,
   Twyford, Wing
Cambridgeshire: Babraham, Bottisham, Harlton, Hildersham,
   Wisbech. *Huntingdon district*: Buckden, Conington, Yaxley
Carmarthenshire: Carmarthen
Cheshire: Acton, Barthomley, Bunbury, Chester (St John),
   Gawsworth, Malpas
Cornwall: Duloe, Kilkhampton, Lanreath, Launceston, St
   Germans, St Ives, St Mellion
Cumbria: Appleby, Cartmel, Lowther
Derbyshire: Ashbourne, Ashover, Ault Hucknall, Bakewell,
   Chesterfield, Hathersage, Norbury
Devon: Bere Ferrers, Branscombe, Colyton, Crediton, East
   Budleigh, Haccombe, Newton St Cyres, Ottery St Mary,
   Payhembury, Shute

Dorset: Beaminster, Bere Regis, Christchurch Priory, Milton Abbas, Sherborne Abbey, Wimborne Minster

Durham: Brancepeth, Chester-le-Street, Norton-on-Tees, Staindrop

Essex: Felsted, Layer Marney, Steeple Bumpstead, Theydon Mount

Gloucestershire: Berkeley, Chipping Campden, Cirencester, Little Barrington, Longborough, Miserden, Sherborne, Westonbirt

Greater Manchester: Bowdon

Hampshire: Catherington, Titchfield

Herefordshire: Bosbury, Clehonger, Eastnor, Holme Lacey, Kinnersley, Moccas, Much Marcle, Ledbury, Weobley

Hertfordshire: Abbots Langley, Aldenham, Berkhamsted, Flamstead, Great Gaddesden, Hatfield, Knebworth, Sawbridgeworth, South Mimms, Tring, Walkern, Wheathampstead

Isle of Wight: Brading, Shorwell, Whippingham

Kent: Borden, Chartham, Cobham, Goudhurst, Lynsted, Maidstone (All Saints), Otford, Penshurst, Shoreham, Tenterden, Waldershare, Wingham

Lancashire: Mitton, Lancaster (St Mary), Rochdale (St Chad), Standish, Whalley

Leicestershire: Ashby-de-la-Zouch, Ashby Folville, Bottesford, Breedon on the Hill, Gaddesby, Peatling Magna, Prestwold, Quorndon, Rothley, Scraptoft, Shepshed, Stapleford, Thurlaston, Wistow

Lincolnshire: Caistor, Marston, Snarford, Spilsby, Stamford (St Martin), Stoke Rochford

London: The City churches of All Hallows-by-the-Tower, St Bartholomew the Great, St Helen Bishopsgate, St Katharine Cree, St Margaret Pattens, St Mary Abchurch, St Michael Cornhill, The Temple Church. *Greater London:* Barking (St Margaret), Charlton (St Luke), Clerkenwell (St James), Harefield (St Mary), Harrow on the Hill (St Mary), Kew Green (St Anne), Little Stanmore (St Lawrence), Petersham (St Peter)

Merseyside: Sefton

Monmouthshire: Abergavenny

Norfolk: Ashwellthorpe, Besthorpe, Blickling, East Harling, Hunstanton (St Mary), Oxborough, Reepham, Stow Bardolph

Northamptonshire: Croughton, Great Brington, King's Sutton, Lowick, Stanford on Avon, Stow-Nine-Churches, Warkton

Northumberland: Cambo, Chillingham, Hartburn, Hexham Priory

Nottinghamshire: Ratcliffe on Soar, Sibthorpe, Strelley, Willoughby-on-the-Wolds

Oxfordshire: Burford, Ewelme, Faringdon, Fyfield, Great Tew, Little Wittenham, Rotherfield Greys, Spelsbury, Stanton Harcourt, Swinbrook, Thame, Yarnton

Powys: Montgomery

Rutland: Exton, Stoke Dry

Shropshire: Burford, Condover, Claverley, Cound, Norton in Hales, Shrewsbury (Holy Cross), Stanton Lacy, Tong

Somerset: Brent Knoll, Churchill, Goathurst, Ilminster, Rodney Stoke, Stogumber, Wellington

Staffordshire: Ashley, Brewood, Croxall, Ilam, Wolverhampton (St Peter)

Suffolk: Boxted, Bures, Culford, Framlingham, Hawstead, Hengrave, Long Melford, Kedington, Redgrave, Rendlesham, Stoke-by-Nayland, Wingfield

Surrey: Bletchingley, Godstone, Great Bookham, Stoke D'Abernon, Wotton

Sussex: Ashburnham, Boxgrove, Rye, Winchelsea, Withyham

Warwickshire: Alcester, Honington, Stratford-upon-Avon, Warwick (St Mary), Wootton Wawen

West Midlands: Binley

Wiltshire: Bradford-on-Avon (Holy Trinity), Edington, Great Bedwyn, Laycock, Lydiard Tregoze, Ramsbury, Tisbury, Urchfont

Worcestershire: Chaddesley Corbett, Croome D'Abitot, Elmley Castle, Great Witley, Strensham, Wickhamford

Yorkshire:

North: Bedale, Coxwold, Guisborough, Hornby

East Riding: Aldingfleet, Beverley Minster, Boynton, Hull (Holy Trinity)

South: Thrybergh, Wentworth old church, Worsbrough

West: Harewood, Kirkheaton, Ledsham, Methley, Otley, Thornhill, Whitkirk

Hatchments, or funeral hatchments

Funeral hatchments are coats-of-arms painted on a wooden panel or canvas frame and attached to a diamond-shaped wooden frame. They are often seen in old churches and usually date from the late seventeenth or eighteenth century, although in some parts of the country the practice continued into the nineteenth century, with the corners of the hatchment decorated with rosettes. Their purpose was associated with a funeral – usually of a member of

A funeral hatchment, St Mark and St Luke, Avington, Berkshire.

the local gentry. The hatchment, a heraldic device, was hung for some months in front of the house of a deceased person and then brought into the church. Some hatchments include initials and a date. The word *'resurgam'* also often appears. It is not a motto of the family but a hopeful statement of belief – 'I will rise again'. The background to a hatchment is either completely black or half-black and half-white according to the married state of the person commemorated. There were set rules for this – for example, a widower would have a black background with the arms divided into two – his own and those of his wife. A married woman who died before her husband would have a background that was half-black and half-white, with the left side white and the right side black. If her husband had died first the background would be reversed. In both cases the arms would be divided into two.

Many churches possess quite a number of hatchments. They are colourful and they usually adorn a wall inside the church.

Sometimes they have been removed to a more obscure corner of the building such as the vestry or the ringing chamber.

At St Nicholas at Stanford-on-Avon, Northamptonshire, there are 17 hatchments on display. There is also a fine array at All Saints, Theydon Garnon, Essex. The practice persists occasionally to this day, although none have been recorded yet in the present century.

Hatchments are sometimes associated with *funeral helmets* or *helms*. These are usually stylized helmets dating from the time of the hatchment. Sometimes when you see an ancient helmet on a church wall on its own it is because the hatchment associated with it is no longer there.

Flags and banners

Three types of flag are to be found inside churches: heraldic flags, military colours and the flags of various local organizations with links to the church, such as the British Legion and branches of the Scout Movement.

A heraldic banner is a square or oblong flag that carries the arms of the person it belongs to. On the death of a knight his personal banner was often, like a hatchment, hung in the parish church.

Seafaring contemporary banner, St Clement, Leigh-on-Sea, Essex.

Military colours are sometimes to be found in churches where there is a strong local military connection and no cathedral. Many of the historic regimental colours have lost most of their original material and what is left is contained in the gauze that protects them.

Local banners are far more common. One of the organizations most likely to have banners of this sort, used for processional purposes, is the Mothers' Union.

In some churches you will also find banners depicting sacred symbols or the patron saint of that particular church. Again, they are generally designed to be carried in procession.

Brass memorials

Don't forget to look beneath your feet for brass memorials and inscriptions as you tour an ancient church. We have about 8,000 of them in this country, as opposed to a few hundred in the whole of Europe and Scandinavia – a magnificent national collection, and nearly all of them available for all to see in our parish churches.

Brasses are incised memorial portraits and inscriptions. Although they are generally set in large flagstones in the church floor they have sometimes been repositioned on church walls, largely to preserve them from damage by the feet of people passing through the building. They are also sometimes to be seen fixed to the top of tomb chests.

You may have to hunt beneath a mat (there is good reason to cover brasses in church floors with pieces of carpet) or in the floor of a pew, or even beneath a piece of furniture, to find a brass mentioned in the guidebook to the church you happen to be exploring.

Brasses are normally engraved with a figure representing the person commemorated, and the figure or figures depicted were usually from the brass engraver's stock. It is very rare to find a portrait brass – one that is a direct representation of the person commemorated.

Heraldry played an important part in brass design, and the various devices were sometimes inlaid with enamel colours, although this can rarely still be seen except in more modern Victorian and twentieth-century church brasses.

Brass memorial to Jane, daughter of Robert Ingylton (1557),
St Michael, Thornborough, Buckinghamshire.

The earliest memorial brasses date from about 1250, although
the finest quality brasses usually date from the following century.
The brasses from this time usually compare very favourably with
anything the Victorians produced. The figures are nearly life-
size and the engraving is much more deeply cut and far more
hand-crafted than the rather mechanical lettering often found in
nineteenth-century brasses.

Fine sepulchral brass,
St Mary, Ufford,
Suffolk (1598).

It is thought that brasses, which are, in fact, made from an alloy of copper, originally came to Britain from the Low Countries. Certainly we know that until the end of the fifteenth century most of the material for making them was imported at great cost from mainland Europe. To have a memorial brass in a church as a form of commemoration was therefore a sign of great wealth. They were usually commissioned during the lifetime of the person to be commemorated.

Church explorers should also be on the lookout for more unusual brasses. Although the vast majority of brasses are inscriptions or depict figures of people, you will also find the occasional pictorial brass or one depicting the Holy Trinity. The latter are usually placed above and between the main figure brasses in a memorial. They usually show God the Father bearded and enthroned, Jesus on the Cross, and the Holy Ghost as a dove with a halo.

The most prolific time for monumental brass creation was during the fifteenth and sixteenth centuries, when wool reigned

Typical mid 14th-century floor brass, St Michael,
Stanton Harcourt, Oxfordshire.

supreme. Some of the best brasses are to be found in the great
'wool churches'. London was the great centre, but there were
workshops in other towns in the southern half of the country and
in East Anglia. There were far fewer in the North, which is the
reason why the greatest concentration of medieval brasses is still
to be found today in churches in the southern half of the country.

Another interesting feature of brasses is that from time to time
they are *palimpsests*. These are brasses that have been used more
than once. Because of the great value of the material it was often

Memorial brass to 'Honest old Thomas Cotes', a faithful retainer, seen kneeling in prayer, hat beside him (1648), All Saints, Wing, Buckinghamshire. Brasses like this would almost certainly have been originally floor-mounted. Fixing it to the wall has meant the use of unsightly nails, which have become disfigured and ruined much of the effect.

used several times over. The usual method was simply to turn the brass over and re-engrave and reset it. However, sometimes the figures themselves were altered, or in some instances retained and the inscription replaced, so the same brass figure then commemorated a different person!

On occasions it is known that one part of an original brass is in one church and the other in a different one. Enthusiasts can usually tell by a detailed knowledge of the dress in different periods – something which might be of interest to many church explorers. On one occasion experts even found two halves of the same original brass – both reused – as far apart as Devon and Suffolk!

When this happens the way experts marry together the different pieces is usually by the dress. This involves the study of every type of armour, civil costume and ladies' dresses and headdresses, as well as priests' vestments and academic and judicial costume of the medieval period, and is the only really accurate means of being able to date a brass.

You will often find the outline of an ancient brass in the stone into which it was obviously set. It may have been stolen, or more likely removed, by Puritan elements during the Cromwellian period.

Monumental brasses lost their popularity as memorials towards the end of the sixteenth century when there was a greater desire for three-dimensional memorials. However, the Gothic Revival in the reign of Queen Victoria brought about a return to the production of monumental brasses. Many workshops were set up, and they even produced catalogues. However, Victorian brasses can nearly always be identified at a glance. Although often of high quality, the execution tends to be less free-flowing and more mechanical. Throughout the twentieth century a slow but steady flow of monumental brasses emerged from the small number of workshops still capable of producing them.

Where to find fine brasses

Most remaining brasses are to be found in the south and south-eastern counties of England. They are particularly fine in centres of the medieval woollen trade such as The Cotswolds, Lincolnshire, Somerset and East Anglia, where there was widespread affluence among the merchant classes in the fifteenth and sixteenth centuries. Wool merchants' brasses can often be identified by their feet resting on a bale of wool and some evidence on the brass of their personal mark, which in life used to be stamped on each bale of wool they handled.

They become fewer as one travels north or/and west, primarily because these were poorer parts of the country. There are few brasses in Wales and even fewer in Scotland.

Fine brasses may be found in:

Bedfordshire: Bromham, Cardington, Cople, Elstow, Wymington

Berkshire: Bray, Cookham, Shottesbrooke

Bristol: (St Mary Redcliffe)

Buckinghamshire: Amersham, Bradenham, Burnham, Chalfont St Giles, Chenies, Denham, Drayton Beauchamp, Nether Winchendon, Pitstone, Taplow, Thornborough, Thornton, Wing

Cambridgeshire: Hildersham, Isleham, Little Shelford, Trumpington, Westley Waterless

Cheshire: Macclesfield, Over, Wilmslow, Winwick

Cornwall: Constantine, St Germans, St Mawgan, St Mellion

Cumbria: Crosthwaite, Edenhall, Great Musgrave, Greystoke, Lowther

Derbyshire: Hathersage, Morley, Tideswell

Devon: Bigbury, Chittlehampton, Dartmouth (St Saviour), Haccombe, Shillingford, Stoke Fleming

Dorset: Thorncombe, Wimborne Minster

Durham: Bishop Auckland, Chester-le-Street, Sedgefield

Essex: Chigwell, Chrishall, Little Easton, Little Horkesley, Pebmarsh, Wivenhoe

Gloucestershire: Chipping Campden, Cirencester, Deerhurst, Dyrham, Fairford, Northleach

Hampshire and Isle of Wight: Freshwater, King's Sombourne, Thruxton

Herefordshire: Brampton Abbotts, Clehonger, Llandinabo, Marden

Hertfordshire: Digswell, Hitchin, Knebworth, North Mymms, Watton-at-Stone

Huntingdon district: Offord D'Arcy, Sawtry

Kent: Chartham, Cobham, East Sutton, Hever, Minster-in-Sheppey

Lancashire: Ormskirk

Leicestershire: Ab Kettleby, Bottesford, Castle Donington, Wanlip

Lincolnshire: Boston, Buslingthorpe, Croft, Linwood, Spilsby, Tattershall

London and Greater London: Beddington, Carshalton, City (All Hallows by the Tower; St Helen, Bishopgate; St Olave, Hart St), Enfield, Harrow, Ruislip

Merseyside: Sefton

Norfolk: Ashwellthorpe, Blickling, East Dereham, East Harling, Elsing, Felbrigg, Hunstanton, King's Lynn (St Margaret), Norwich (St John, Maddermarket), Rougham

Northamptonshire: Ashby St Ledgers, Castle Ashby, Higham Ferrers, Geddington, Lowick

Northumberland: Hexham

Nottinghamshire: East Markham, Newark, Strelley

Oxfordshire: Blewbury, Brightwell Baldwin , Buckland, Childrey, Chinnor, Cumnor, Denchworth, Dorchester, Stanton Harcourt, Swinbrook, Thame, Wantage, Waterperry, West Hanney, Witney

Rutland: Exton, Little Casterton

Shropshire: Acton Burnell, Tong

Somerset: Ilminster, South Petherton, Yeovil

Staffordshire: Audley, Okeover

Suffolk: Acton, Burgate, Long Melford, Mendlesham, Playford, Stoke-by-Nayland, Yoxford

Surrey: East Horsley, Lingfield, Stoke D'Abernon, Thames Ditton

Sussex: Amberley , Cowfold, Etchingham, Trotton, West Grinstead, Wiston

Tyne & Wear: Newcastle upon Tyne (All Saints; St Nicholas)

Wales: Beaumaris, Llanover, Llanrwst, Swansea (St Mary)

Warwickshire: Baginton, Merevale, Warwick (St Mary), Wellesbourne, Wixford

Wiltshire: Bromham, Draycot Cerne, Mere, Tisbury

Worcestershire: Fladbury, Kidderminster, Strensham

Yorkshire: Aldborough, Bainton, Brandsburton, Harewood, Harpham, Ledsham, Topcliffe, Wensley

Good twentieth-century brasses may be found in:

Devon: Exeter (St David)
Kent: Kemsing
Surrey: Guildford (St Nicholas)

Royal Arms

You will find these on the walls of many parish churches. They are generally painted on wood, canvas or plaster and set on a square background. However, some of the finest are hand-carved in wood. The practice of displaying Royal Arms in churches is

Royal arms of King James I, St Andrew, West Stafford, Dorset.

believed to have started in the reign of King Henry VIII, who was, for obvious reasons, keen to put his stamp on the newly founded Church of England after the break with Rome. Royal Arms in churches gradually increased in number under Elizabeth I, James I and Charles I. In 1660, with the Restoration of Charles II, it became compulsory to display them in every parish church above the chancel arch. Today nearly all the Royal Arms to be seen in churches date from the reign of Charles II or later. You will sometimes still find them above the chancel arch, but generally they will have been moved to other positions.

A small number of Royal Arms were installed in churches in the twentieth century. At least five of these were in the reign of our present Queen, Elizabeth II.

PART 4

The Churchyard

8

What to Look For in the Churchyard

Beneath these rugged elms, that yew tree's shade,
Where heaves the turf in many a mouldering heap,
Each in his narrow cell for ever laid
The rude forefathers of the hamlet sleep.
Thomas Gray (1716–77)

Before you leave the church and its surroundings, don't forget to take a final look around the churchyard. It may well contain some things of interest.

Things to look out for

First of all note the *shape* of the churchyard. It is thought that many churchyards originated as circular shapes – partly because this was the most obvious shape to circumnavigate a building but also because many churches were established on previously pagan sites, which were often round. These might not necessarily have been burial places, but certainly places associated with religious ritual or ceremonies. To know that the church you have been visiting stands on a site that has been used for worship of some sort since time immemorial is of interest to many church explorers.

Circular churchyards

Bedfordshire: Stagsden
Buckinghamshire: Edlesborough, Lavendon
Derbyshire: Wirksworth
Dorset: Knowlton
East Riding of Yorkshire: Rudston

Essex: Steeple Bumpstead, Wixoe
Northamptonshire: Winwick
Oxfordshire: East Hendred, Letcombe Regis
Powys: Old Radnor,

Churchyards with two churches

Cambridgeshire: Swaffham Prior
Essex: Willingale
Lincolnshire: Alvingham, North Cockerington
Norfolk: Antingham, Great Melton, Reepham, South Walsham
Suffolk: Trimley
Worcestershire: Evesham

Churches on the site of prehistoric forts or encampments

Berkshire: Finchampstead
Buckinghamshire: West Wycombe
Cornwall: Kilkhampton, Mawnan
Devon: Brentor
Dorset: Knowlton
Herefordshire: Brinsop
Kent: Coldred
Leicestershire: Breedon on the Hill, Burton Overy, Melling
Northamptonshire: Lilbourne
Suffolk: Burgh
Warwickshire: Brinklow
Wiltshire: Avebury

Many ancient churchyards have been overtaken by urban development so that today it is very hard to tell the original shape, particularly because rises in population may have caused more land to be absorbed for burials.

Historical activities in churchyards

Although we generally associate churchyards with peace and calm it was not always so. Burials there might have been, but churchyards were also used for fencing, wrestling, cock-fighting, quoins, ninepins and ball games. In medieval times there were dancing and events called 'church ales' in churchyards; fairs were held, and travelling merchants set up their booths and stalls. Sometimes bells were cast in churchyards because of the perils of travel and the difficulties of transporting heavy loads. Even Civil War skirmishes sometimes took place in churchyards. Alton in Hampshire was a case in point, and at Burford in Oxfordshire and Painswick in Gloucestershire it is still possible to see bullet marks in the exterior walls of the churches.

As a church explorer you could try and find evidence of all these activities. It is not easy. However, at Martock in Somerset, for example, it is still possible to see what are said to be the footholds in the stonework of the church, made so that balls could be retrieved from the roof. And at Craswall in Herefordshire it is still just possible to spot a levelled area by the north wall of the chancel where Fives was played.

Archery

If you should see a sign saying 'The Butts' near an ancient church, this will almost certainly indicate that archery practice took place within or very near the churchyard.

In 1466, in the reign of Edward IV there was an edict decreeing that every able-bodied Englishman should have a longbow of his own height and practice regularly at the butts.

Don't forget that many churches were built within the outer precincts of castles or fortified houses, and that these were also places where archers traditionally practised. The castle may no longer be there, but the church might remain. Some splendid examples of this can be seen in the Welsh borders, perhaps the best being Richards Castle near Ludlow.

Churches in wonderful situations

Buckinghamshire: Edlesborough, Penn
Cheshire: Delamere
Cornwall: Mylor, St Just-in-Roseland, St Winnow
Cumbria: Alston, Bromfield, Grasmere, Great Ormside, Lanercost, Morland, Mungrisdale, Ulpha, Waberthwaite
Derbyshire: Woodhead
Devon: Brentor, Countisbury
Dorset: Milton Abbas, St Adhelms, Winterborne Tomson, Worth Matravers
Essex: Willingale
Gloucestershire: Chedworth, Painswick
Hampshire: Portchester, Silchester
Kent: Bobbing, Frindsbury
Leicestershire: Breedon on the Hill, Eaton, Thornton
Norfolk: Blakeney, Cley, Hales, Wiveton
Northamptonshire: Brampton Ash, Fotheringhay
Northumberland: Bolam, Brinkburn
Oxfordshire: Ewelme
Shropshire: Hope Bagot, Kenley, Melverley, Prees
Somerset: Minehead, Selworthy
Staffordshire: Stourton
Suffolk: Blythburgh, Lavenham, Long Melford
Sussex: Wisborough Green, Herstmonceux
Warwickshire: Merevale, Rowington, Tamworth-in-Arden, Wootton Wawen, Wormleighton
Worcestershire: Arley
Yorkshire: Hubberholme, Grinton, Patrington, West Tanfield, Whitby

Yew trees

The connection between archery and all those ancient churchyard yews is far more tenuous. The idea that the timber was grown for longbows has fallen out of favour. After all, why churchyards? Couldn't yew trees have been grown anywhere? Besides, we know that English yew was generally considered less suitable than that

Ancient churchyard yew that now serves a useful purpose!
St Bartholomew, Much Marcle, Herefordshire.

from Spain and Portugal, so many have searched elsewhere for a reason for the ubiquitous churchyard yew.

An alternative explanation is that since the leaves of the yew are poisonous and eating them in any quantity would probably mean death to domestic animals, priests had yews planted in churchyards to force local farmers to protect their stock by keeping churchyard fencing secure at their own expense rather than that of the church.

However, this theory conflicts with the fact that stock were often herded into churchyards in times of attack for protective purposes: hence the high walls, traces of which mark the boundaries of many ancient churchyards.

What is known is that some churchyard yews are more than 1,000 years old, and that because they are capable of self-regeneration they were venerated by the Celts for their apparent immortality. They are therefore symbols, rather like the green man that we often see carved high into the walls of churches, of rebirth and the immortality of nature.

Throughout the medieval period Christians continued to use yew branches as symbols of everlasting life in processions and ceremonies.

Churchyards with fine old yew trees

Berkshire: Aldworth
Derbyshire: Darley Dale, Doveridge
Devon: Bampton
Dorset: Woolland
Gloucestershire: Painswick
Greater London: Cudham
Hampshire: Brockenhurst, Corhampton, Selborne, South Hayling
Herefordshire: Linton, Much Marcle
Kent: Capel St Thomas, Elmstead, Stelling, Ulcombe
Monmouthshire: Bettws-Newydd
Powys: Llanfihangel
Surrey: Crowhurst, Hambledon, Tandridge
Sussex: Crowhurst
Wiltshire: Tisbury

Churchyard crosses

Whereas ancient yews are generally found in the southern half of the country, ancient *churchyard crosses* are more common in what are generally known as the 'Celtic Fringes' – the areas to which the ancient British tribes were driven by the waves of invading Danes. Church explorers will therefore see the highest numbers of them in Wales, Cornwall and northern England. The ancient Celtic wheel-head symbol predates the church as we know it, which was refounded by St Augustine in or near Canterbury in 597. The shape is thought to have originated in the Mediterranean region.

The straightforward churchyard cross – the ancient symbol of Christ crucified – is believed to have developed from the simple wooden crosses that were used from the sixth century onwards to mark places of worship and were probably a follow-on from the wooden crosses or staffs carried by early Christian missionaries.

Nevertheless, churchyard crosses may be a continuation of yet another of those ancient pagan symbols, the standing stone, which were 'Christianized' by the early missionaries from Rome around the time of St Augustine. In the churchyard at Rudston, North Yorkshire, there is a stone monolith nearly 26 feet high – the tallest standing stone in Britain.

Where to find early stone crosses:

Cheshire: Halton, Prestbury, Sandbach

Cornwall: Cardinham, Feock, Lamorran, Lanhydrock, Lanivet, Launceston, Lostwithiel, Mylor, Padstow, Par, Phillack, Porthilly, Roche, St Allen, St Buryan, St Clement, St Dennis, St Ives, St Juliot, St Mawgan, St Neot, St Teath, Sancreed, Wendron

Cumbria: Beckermet St Bridget, Bewcastle, Burton-in-Kendal, Dacre, Dearham, Gosforth, Heversham, Kirkby Stephen, Ireton

Derbyshire: Bakewell, Brailsford, Eyam, Hope

Dumfries and Galloway: Ruthwell

Dyfed: Nevern

Lancashire: Hornby, Heysham, Whalley

Leicestershire: Rothley, Sproxton

Lincolnshire: Creeton

Nottinghamshire: Stapleford

Staffordshire: Alstonfield, Checkley, Ilam, Leek, Rolleston

Yorkshire: Hauxwell, Masham, Nunburnholme

Medieval churchyard crosses

Medieval churchyard crosses are altogether different. They traditionally represented the only memorial to all the unmarked graves, and so were positioned in a prominent position in the churchyard. When you see an old churchyard cross of this sort it is usually a *tabernacle* cross, with an enlarged – or lantern – head, originally designed to contain images of Our Lady and Child and

a crucifix. The alternative was a straightforward *cross head* or *cross shaft* cross.

Unless they have been reconstructed, very few of these complete crosses remain. Many were destroyed by Cromwell's soldiers during the Civil War. Others have been worn away by the ravages of time. However, many medieval crosses of this type remain as just a base and a shaft. When you see an ancient cross of this kind that looks complete, take a look at the base. If the upper sections look newer than the base, then this is probably the sole remaining ancient section.

Contemporary tabernacle cross in an Oxfordshire churchyard.

Where to find medieval stone crosses:

Cambridgeshire: Croxton
Dorset: Rampisham
Essex: Castle Hedingham
Gloucestershire: Ampney Crucis, Ashleworth, Didmarton, Iron
   Acton, North Cerney
Herefordshire: Blakemere, Bosbury, Ross-on-Wye, Tyberton,
   Weobley
Lincolnshire: Alkborough, Somersby, Tattershall
Monmouthshire: Grosmont
Northamptonshire: Higham Ferrers
Oxfordshire: Iffley, North Hinksey
Shropshire: Bitterley, Highley, Ightfield
Somerset: Bishop's Lydeard, Chewton Mendip, Crowcombe
Wiltshire: Bremhill, Cricklade
Worcestershire: Great Malvern, Ombersley
Yorkshire: Ripley

Lychgates

The name lychgate is derived from the Anglo-Saxon word *lich*, meaning 'corpse'. This refers to the days when a structure was needed to provide shelter for shrouded bodies until the arrival of the priest, at a time when coffins were not common.

People always seem to assume that lychgates were originally designed as places where the coffin bearers could rest after having carried the coffin a long distance. Although this is true in part, as with so many matters concerning churches, there is more to it than that.

In the Prayer Book of 1549 it was laid down that the priest should meet the funeral procession at the entrance to the church-yard and conduct the beginning of the burial service there. From there the procession moved on to the porch for the second stage of the service, and thence to the chancel for the final solemnities before burial in the churchyard.

Some lychgates are long and grandiose, and incorporate seats

Lychgate with coffin stone, St Michael and All Angels,
Kington St Michael, Wiltshire.

along their length, while others, like the ones at Friston in East
Sussex, at Duntisbourne Abbots and North Cerney, both in
Gloucestershire, and at Hayes in Greater London, have a swivel-
ling mechanism, designed to make the passage of a coffin easier.

Some lychgates have two storeys, the upper storey having been
originally designed as a schoolroom, parish store, priest's room or
library.

Churchyards with unusual or ancient lychgates

Berkshire: Bray
Buckinghamshire: Chalfont St Giles, Stoke Poges, Weston Turville
Cornwall: Feock, Kenwyn, St Clement, Wendron
Cumbria: Troutbeck
Devon: Ilsington
Gloucestershire: North Cerney, Painswick
Greater London: Beckenham
Hampshire: East Meon
Herefordshire: Monnington on Wye
Hertfordshire: Anstey, Ashwell
Kent: Boughton Monchelsea, Igtham
Leicestershire: Bitteswell
Lincolnshire: Fleet
North Yorkshire: Burnsall
Pembrokeshire: Stackpole
Shropshire: Clun
Surrey: Betchworth, Limpsfield, Shere
Sussex: Bolney, Friston
Warwickshire: Long Compton
Wiltshire: Downton, Wanborough
Worcestershire: Bockleton , Overbury

Cemeteries

Cemeteries are separate from churches, and although some village cemeteries can share the quality of churchyards, the order of scale means that they often lack the character of ancient churchyards, which have grown organically over the centuries. Large cemeteries were very often a response to the growth of urban populations in the nineteenth century, before cremation became customary in the inter-war period. The great Victorian cemeteries can be fascinating and beautiful places, although all too often many years of inattention have left many of them in a sad state, with layers of neglect and repeated vandalism having taken their toll.

Overgrown Victorian cemetery, Leicester.

Holy wells

You will also probably spot that the word w*ell* appears in English place-names a great deal, and this opens up another area for church explorers. Although today the places where an ancient holy well is to be found are very few in number, it is clear that many churches were originally associated with these water sources. Such sites were venerated in pagan times, just as they were by the Romans, so again we often find a continuity of worship that probably dates back to well before Christian times.

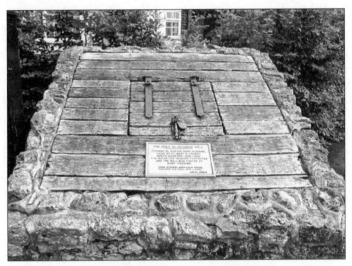

Holy well, associated with the 14th-century rector John Schorne, North Marston, Buckinghamshire.

The most obvious places to go hunting for ancient holy wells are in the Celtic fringes, namely, Cornwall and Wales, where the names of many obscure Celtic saints are associated with these water cults. The most famous now is the Roman Catholic shrine at Holywell in North Wales. It is still a place of pilgrimage and is sometimes referred to as the 'Lourdes of Wales'.

At Berkswell in West Midlands the church of St John sits on a site thought to date back to the Dark Ages. The ancient spring just outside the gate was once dedicated to a Saxon deity and the base of the churchyard cross is thought to have been the base for a statue of that god.

There is a similar arrangement at North Marston in Buckinghamshire, where the well and the shrine of the fourteenth-century rector, John Schorne, were visited for many years by pilgrims seeking a cure for gout. Schorne, regarded by many in his day as a saint, claimed to have imprisoned the Devil in a boot, thus enabling him to cure gout. The well is now kept covered. For the church explorer the interest of these ancient sites is in uncovering hints and clues as to where other holy wells existed that were undoubtedly a key part of early worship.

Unusual churchyard buildings

These vary from the splendid little stone priest's houses at Elkstone in Gloucestershire, and Itchingfield in Sussex, to the school buildings of Burgh in Suffolk, Thursley in Surrey and Wraxall in Somerset, and to ancient lockups, as the one at Bromham in Wiltshire. At Mere, also in Wiltshire, there is an ancient charnel house, a building where bones from reused graves were stored.

Church houses do not always appear in churchyards, but always in association with the church. They are a West Country speciality. Really they were the precursors of what we call *church halls* today. They were used for activities connected with the church: often church ales and other celebratory events. Some have been converted into private houses or pubs: others are still in use for much of their original purpose. Good examples are at Crowcombe in Somerset, and at Harberton Braunton, Walkhampton and South Tawton, all in Devon.

Churchyard oddities

There are two standing stones, one of known pagan origin, in the churchyard at Rudston in East Riding of Yorkshire.

At Braunstone churchyard in Leicestershire there is a carved figure which appears to be a pagan fertility symbol and which may have been an object of worship there in pre-Christian times.

At Stanhope, County Durham, there is a fossilized tree-stump

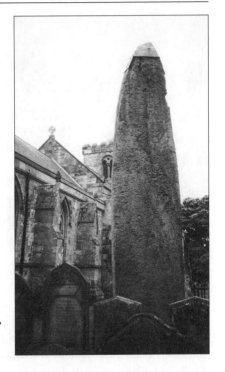

Large standing stone in the churchyard, All Saints, Rudston, East Riding of Yorkshire.

estimated to be 250 million years old. It was dug out of a local quarry and now stands by the church wall.

In the churchyard at Otley, West Yorkshire, there is an enormous communal gravestone in the form of a castellated model of a railway tunnel commemorating the men killed in the construction of a Yorkshire tunnel in the years 1845–9.

Surely the most unusual churchyard monument must be at Brightling in East Sussex. There the squire and nineteenth-century MP for East Sussex, John ('Mad Jack') Fuller (1757–1834) chose to be interred in a 25-foot high pyramid in the churchyard. Today it is a local landmark.

The churchyard at Painswick, Gloucestershire, contains 99 yew trees, some of which are well over 200 years old.

Many ancient churchyards are higher, at least on one side, than the floor level of the churches they serve. This is usually because of many layers of burials. In some cases the land has risen so much

Some of the 99 yew trees at Painswick, Gloucestershire, with stone table tombs in the foreground.

that the main path to the church resembles a small-scale railway cutting, with the ground piled on either side. In many churches you step down into the porch, or the main structure of the building: again this is often because the churchyard level has risen as a result of repeated layers of burials.

The dark side of the churchyard

In medieval times a highly superstitious congregation believed that the Devil, although excluded from the church itself, still existed in the churchyard, particularly in the shadow of the north side. For this reason, even in the eighteenth century when gravestones were in common use, there was a strong preference to be buried on the south side, and the north side was still reserved for undesirables such as unbaptized infants, criminals and suicides.

This is the reason why, even today, you will generally find fewer burials on the north side of a churchyard, and it is still the practice to bury the dead on an east–west alignment with the head to the east, a throwback to the days of pagan worship, when the sun god – the source of all light – rose in the east.

Body-snatching

The gruesome trade of body-snatching was at its height in the second half of the eighteenth century, when increasing medical research required the dissection of human corpses for the training of surgeons. The law permitted the London medical schools to acquire the corpses of executed murderers, but demand exceeded supply and a trade in corpses developed. To deter body-snatching, which was not a crime until legislation in 1831 finally put an end to it, special watch huts were constructed in many churchyards. At Pannal in Yorkshire an immense medieval stone coffin was hired out by the fortnight and positioned over freshly dug graves to stop body-snatching. At Frenchay in Gloucestershire a huge stone used for the same purpose is still to be seen in the Unitarian graveyard. In other churchyards 'body-snatchers cages' were used. These were iron grills erected round the graves and later moved on for use elsewhere when the corpses would have been too decayed to be of use for medical research.

Watchmen's huts, where all-night guards were positioned to deter body-snatchers, are still to be seen in the churchyards at Warblington in Hampshire and Morpeth in Northumberland.

The churchyard as a nature reserve

Today there is much emphasis on using churchyards, particularly those in urban areas, as 'green spaces' where, under minimal control, nature can be allowed to have its way. The practice, widespread in the 1950s, 1960s and 1970s, of levelling a churchyard, or a large area of a churchyard to create an easily-mowed lawn, with the headstones parked round the outside ('like playing cards' as John Betjeman remarked in his poem 'Churchyards') is now widely discouraged.

Nowadays most Church of England dioceses will generally approve only limited clearance schemes for memorials that are broken and defaced, between 50 and 70 years after the burial. Even then there first has to be a lengthy process of consultation. The churchyard you are about to explore should therefore be a wildlife haven – if you know what to look for.

In order to appreciate it to the full you might wish to contact an organization called Caring for God's Acre (see Appendix 3),

Levelled churchyard at Quenington, Gloucestershire.

which provides advice about both how to look for these things and how to manage churchyards.

Organizations such as this encourage sensitive management, so that while burials in recent years are kept tidy, older areas of the churchyard are allowed to remain as what is known as 'semi-natural grassland' – a species-rich habitat with a predominance of long meadow grasses and native meadow plants.

Old headstones also have an ecology of their own. The differing blends of grey, green and yellow lichens that grow on old headstones are immensely sensitive plants and need very precise conditions in which to grow. That is why churchyard enthusiasts take delight in finding different lichen species on the front, back and tops of headstones.

Many churchyard enthusiasts become involved in flora and fauna surveys run under the auspices of their local wildlife trusts.

Birds love the cover afforded by churchyards, and some species, like house sparrows or the swifts, which swirl and dip around the tower, make their homes in the church building. More unusual birds can also be seen. Some, like the tree creeper, nest inside loose bark, while woodpeckers make their nests within the trunks. The trees in churchyards provide food for many species of insects, which in turn feed a variety of birds.

The spotted flycatcher, a summer migrant, is often to be seen in churchyards, which are an important habitat for them because of their excellent supply of insects for food and their wide open spaces with plenty of places to perch.

Lichen on stone table tombs, Standish, Gloucestershire.

Even in towns, churchyards provide good entertainment for bird enthusiasts.

Foxes, deer and snakes can also be observed in forgotten churchyard corners where the grass has been allowed to grow. At some times of the year you should be able to observe all manner of butterflies and also a large number of small mammals. Amongst the tree roots and in the boles of the larger trees, and along the hedges, woodmice may thrive, as well as shrews, bank voles and hedgehogs.

More controversial are the large colonies of bats to be found hunting in churchyards, because they often use the surrounding church buildings as a roost. Before they set out at dusk to hunt, a bat will try to lose as much of his bodyweight as possible by defecating. Hence the presence of bat droppings inside many a church. This can cause an understandable problem for church cleaners. Conservationists, however believe that bats, which are protected mammals, should be left to use churches as they need to.

Bats also sometimes roost in church porches, while swallows frequently like to nest in there.

Gravestones and memorials

Trawling churchyards for memorial stones to one's ancestors is a hugely popular pastime today. However, church monuments are interesting for all sorts of other reasons.

For a start, they tell you a great deal about the community. For example, at an old churchyard near the sea you are likely to find many headstones commemorating people who have drowned. Local historians conducting research, for example, into a particular industry that may have thrived in the nineteenth century in a certain area, will almost certainly derive useful information from headstones. Such stones are also of use to genealogists and archaeologists and are in themselves a legacy to the skills of our ancestors.

Above all, headstones document the lives of people who have lived, and often worked, in the parish. So if you are unable to get into the church and have taken a good look round the structure from the outside, the headstones and memorials in the churchyard may provide a great deal to catch your interest.

Some church explorers are particularly keen on visiting churchyards where famous people are buried. Details of books that will help are given in Appendix 4 – Further Reading.

On entering the graveyard, try to pick out any very early stones. These are likely to be near the church and will be few in number because the practice of erecting headstones did not become widespread until the seventeenth century. Early headstones or grave markers are small and plain, and usually primitively carved. A number of churchyards have examples of surviving early medieval coffins hewn from huge blocks of stone.

These would have been buried so that the top, often decorated with a heraldic design, was on a level with the ground. However, if you find a memorial or stone inscribed with a date much before 1600 you will have quite a rare find on your hands. The fact, it seems, is that gradually the insides of the churches filled up with burials and memorials and that the pressure on space became so great that it was impossible to continue interring local people of high status inside the building. The result was that they were buried outside, preferably as near to the church walls as possible. The usual practice with these outside burials was to emulate the large flat slabs known as 'ledger stones', still seen widely

Churchyard memorial to Tiddles, the church cat (1963–80), Fairford, Gloucestershire.

inside churches dating from the beginning of the seventeenth century.

The 'Golden Age' of letter-cutting was in the period between about 1700 and 1850, the best headstones being Georgian, dating from about 1715 through to about 1840. The lettering at this time was bold, incisive and well-formed: vastly superior to what followed when Victorian mechanization took over.

The earlier seventeenth-century stones are plainer and have less decoration. They tend to be short and thick in relation to their height, and generally have flat heads, except for where a scroll forms the shoulders.

Headstones of this period are often amusing, particularly in country areas, because words often run together without proper spacing, producing a quaint and often droll effect. Only the width of the stone, it seems, imposed any order on the layout of the masons, who, we have to assume, were builders rather than specialist letter-carvers, and often could not understand all the words they were carving.

Towards the end of the seventeenth century and in the following century the influence of Classical art gradually made itself felt. The result was that more decoration started creeping in. Well-fed cherubs can be seen trumpeting on high their victory over death.

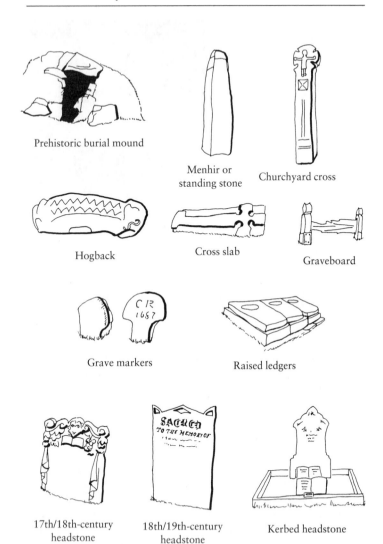

Prehistoric burial mound

Menhir or
standing stone

Churchyard cross

Hogback

Cross slab

Graveboard

Grave markers

Raised ledgers

17th/18th-century
headstone

18th/19th-century
headstone

Kerbed headstone

Gravestones, tombs and monuments.

Body stones

Table tomb

Table tomb

Bale tomb

Cotswold table tomb

Pedestal tomb

Mausoleum

Greek Revival tomb

Monument

Modern maritime
monument

'Tea caddy' tombs are seen here alongside flat-topped table tombs in this Cotswold churchyard.

By the late eighteenth century the fashion for Classical drapery had emerged, along with voluptuous angels – the centrepieces of tableaux amongst shells, urns and symbolism of many other sorts. Angels' features grew more cherubic, and the urn predominated, usually at the head of the stone, with swags of fruit and flowers. Many people prefer the Neo-Classical approach, which is more restrained, and found largely in areas and regions where there was stone that could easily be carved into good memorials. Table tombs are not to be confused with *tomb chests* (see pages 186, 191) and mark a place of burial inside a church. Tomb chests are those great big stone creations that are often (but not always) surmounted by an effigy of the person being commemorated. They are usually free standing.

Classical-style table tombs and the variants of these – bale tombs and the tea caddy tombs – are at their best in the church-yards of the Cotswolds and surrounding 'stone' areas. Other 'regional specialities', such as cast-iron gravestones, are found in several parts of Kent and Sussex and also Shropshire, where there was little freestone, and iron smelting had been carried out for many years. Occasionally, where it survives, you might also find

*Elaborate three-decker
'bale' tomb, Shipton-
under-Wychwood,
Oxfordshire.*

*Late 17th-century table tomb with deeply incised side panels,
Haresfield, Gloucestershire.*

Elaborate late 17th- and 18th-century gravestones, including table tombs, Painswick, Gloucestershire.

the remains of a wooden graveboard in other areas where stone was hard to obtain. These painted boards were also used in stone areas to mark the graves of poorer people whose families could not afford stone memorials. They are rare, however, for two reasons. The first is the obvious one of decay. The second is that if people could not afford a gravestone they would probably not have had a marked grave at all. In the seventeenth and eighteenth centuries the majority of people were buried without any kind of grave marker.

From the 1830s onwards churchyard memorials take on an increasingly mechanical character, even though they may include vigorous and highly decorated letter forms. The surfaces of stones become flat and less attractive and the wording of the inscriptions becomes more impersonal and far less idiosyncratic. This was the age when funerals and mourning were an elaborate and highly elongated process, a fashion set in train by the death of Prince Albert in 1861.

Two fine contemporary headstones commissioned from Memorials by Artists (01728 688934). The tall one in slate is by John Das Gupta, and the 'split boulder' lower stone by Celia Kilner. Photographs by Oliver Riviere.

When it came to the carving of the inscriptions it was very often the case that the work of the local man, with his regional peculiarities of style and rustic lettering, gave way to standard typefaces and designs offered in the catalogues of monumental masons. One can see the profit motive and the materialism of the age constantly creeping in. The Victorians also liked value for money and permanence, and so instead of using the wide variety of English stone available they preferred harder stones like granite and marble, which could by then be cheaply imported. These could take on a glossy polish and could be regularly scrubbed and cleaned. This was completely unlike the softer English stones that would weather gradually, and eventually disintegrate.

The Victorians were also keen to emphasize the idea of ownership and privacy of the grave plot. Graves acquired kerbs, cast-iron rails and even fences. The larger and more flamboyant ones boasted angels, fruit, flags, Classical urns and all manner of figurework and other adornment that today we consider overdone and bordering on the vulgar. Nowadays the church explorer, wandering through a graveyard with a large number of Victorian burials, is likely to be more attracted by the simplicity of the earlier generations of headstone and the native stones that crumble away, almost in tandem, one feels, with the fading memories. Dust to dust . . .

Churchyard authorities are still trying to cast off this Victorian legacy, and to return to a more simple, tasteful approach to memorials and to the choice of suitable stones. In the past 20 or 30 years there has been a marked return to the use of native stones, and to the hand of man rather than the work of the machine. In the best, and most personal, headstones the design is often deeply incised, and carved in high relief. It might also provide some indication of the occupation or interests of the person. For example, in a churchyard in Oxfordshire the stone commemorating a ten-year-old who died in a road accident has a pet rabbit carved on it. And in a churchyard in Dorset the headstone commemorating a keen gardener and vegetable grower has carrots cut into the side bearing the inscription and a spade cut into the rear. Seeking out inspired modern headstones like this can be rewarding for the church explorer who enjoys wandering round churchyards. (See in Appendix 2, 'Memorials by Artists', in the Churchyards section.)

PART 5

Access

9

How Do I Get In?

The church was locked, so I went to the incumbent –
the incumbent enjoyed a supine incumbency –
a tennis court, a summerhouse, deckchairs by the walnut tree
and only the hum of the bees in the rockery.
'May I have the keys of the church, your incumbency?'
John Betjeman

For the church explorer nothing is more galling than to travel a long way and find that the church you wish to see is locked. There are many glories to perceive from the outside, but if you are unable to gain access you may feel your trip is largely wasted.

However, if you are unable to enter the church you are visiting don't give up! Parts 1 and 4 have been deliberately designed to underline some of the pleasures to be gained from a detailed look at the outside and a tour of the churchyard.

Most churches, if they are closed on some days of the week, have a keyholder scheme for visitors, with the names of people who hold keys posted on the church noticeboard or in the porch.

However, this system is by no means perfect – for several reasons. Keyholders cannot always be on hand to answer the phone, and, if the

St Bartholomew's
Church, Yarnton

THIS CHURCH IS

OPEN

Every day from around 10am-4pm

Please feel free to use this place of worship
for your own private prayer, and as a quiet
place to contemplate.

Visitors are most welcome to come and
share in the heritage and living tradition of
the Church of Jesus Christ, Our Saviour, in
this place for the past millennium.

response is an answerphone message, not all visitors are able to wait for a reply. All this, of course, presupposes church visitors all have mobile phones and that they have a good signal.

In addition to this, keyholder signs can be (and are) stolen, in the same way as churches are subject to minor vandalism as well as the occasional theft.

Theft from churches is a big subject, and many new church explorers do not realize the extent of the problem. But minor vandalism is far more common than major theft, and it is understandable if from time to time the officials might think the pru-

dent thing is to close their church for a while until the spate of vandalism is perceived to have died down.

Major theft is a different issue. There is a strong school of thought that says a church that is locked all week gives 'Monday thieves' four clear days to get their booty away and if necessary out of the country before the theft is discovered. Probably more significant than this is the fact that in recent years several police authorities have reported that there are four times as many thefts from locked churches as from open ones. In other words, by the very fact of visiting open churches, church explorers are providing the best protection possible and helping to keep them open.

In addition the Ecclesiastical Insurance Group, which insures 75 per cent of all Anglican churches, insists that it never threatens or charges higher premiums for unlocked churches. So if you find that a church states on its noticeboard that it is closed for 'insurance reasons' you are quite within your rights to make a polite phone call challenging this – especially if it is possible to find out if that particular church is insured with Ecclesiastical.

Having said that, finding volunteers to open and close isolated country churches – there are reckoned to be about 650 in rural Norfolk alone – can be very difficult. At the same time, a locked church is not a welcoming church. Simon Jenkins comments in his excellent *England's Thousand Best Churches*, 'A church shut except for services is the private meeting house of a sect.' In addition, a locked church will not attract donations from visitors. By contrast, an open church will encourage visitors to leave a generous donation in the wall safe. This, in turn, will help to ensure that churches are kept in good condition and open.

Despite such uneven patterns of opening, church-visiting is well-established. Approximately half the 50 Anglican dioceses in England and Wales have a tourism officer. There are 'church trails' locked into tourism schemes in many parts of the country, and all dioceses welcome visitors to their churches. For this reason Appendix 3 includes a list of telephone numbers of diocesan offices in England and Wales. These phones are manned from Monday to Friday, and from the switchboard operator you should be able to obtain details of the diocesan tourism officer, if there is one, and details of either the incumbent or the church-wardens of any of the churches you propose to visit. In this way you should be able to obtain information on the opening times and keyholders pertaining to churches you wish to visit.

If you can use this information to plan your church exploring trips in advance, then this obviously makes sense. However, one of the great joys of church exploring is wandering in an uplanned fashion round an area that is new to you. As with so many things it is hard to have it all ways.

A sensible approach – albeit something of a compromise – is to plan your day around a group of churches within a fairly wide area and be prepared to expect one or two to be closed. Then when you find yourself occasionally thwarted think of all the wonderful churches you have yet to visit, and move on, saying a quiet prayer for those who have kept you out of their churches.

In 1993 Andrew (now Lord) Lloyd Webber acknowledged the problem of gaining access to churches when pursuing his passion for church architecture in many parts of the country. The result was the Open Churches Trust, which for 12 years has been campaigning for as many as possible of the best English and Welsh parish churches, and in some instances other places of worship, to be open for the public to enjoy. Its ultimate aim is that all parish churches should be open so that anyone can wander in and out at will.

The Trust has funded church tourism schemes and in some cases given grants to specific churches in order to aid them to keep the building open. It helps to update parochial church councils throughout England and Wales on measures to protect their property. Usually it does this by regional presentations – generally known as Open Churches Trust Roadshows – to churchwardens and their equivalent in other faiths all over the country. Most Anglican dioceses now participate in the scheme. The

St Mark, Harrogate.

Trust claims significant success: in 1994 it found the ratio of locked to open churches in England and Wales was 3:5 locked all week. Today the figure is closer to 1.5:5. Admittedly many churches have limited opening hours, but all those in the scheme undertake to make it clear to visitors how they might obtain the key at all reasonable hours should the church be closed.

Its website, www.openchurchestrust.org.uk, provides further details of the work of the Trust and also details and opening times of all the churches involved in the scheme.

Appendix 1

Listing of Churches in Scotland

All Saints, Inveraray
   Bell tower memorial to WWI.
Auld Kirk of Killbirnie : W
   Nave from 1470.
Brechin Cathedral: F, G, M
Cathedral of the Isle, Millport, North Ayrshire: G
Dalmeny Parish Church, Edinburgh: D, W
Fenwick Parish Church: M
   Shape of Greek cross.
Haroldswick Methodist, Unst, Shetland
   Norwegian origins.
   Most northerly church in UK.
Iona Abbey
   9th-century, Augustinian nunnery ruins.
The Italian Chapel, Orkney: G
   Built by Italian prisoners of war in the Italian style.
Old Seminary, Scalan
   Catholic seminary now a Farmhouse.
Rosslyn Chapel: W
   Stone carving, famous Prentice pillar.
St Athernase, Leuchars, Fife
   Norman.
St Giles Cathedral, Edinburgh: G
   15th/16th century, Thistle chapel.
St Macher's Cathedral, Aberdeen: M, R, WP
St Salvador, Dundee: WP
St Ternan, Arbuthnott
   13th–15th century origins.
Stobo Kirk
   12th century.

Appendix 2

List of Churches by County

All churches are worth a visit, and everyone will have their own favourites. The list here includes a great many of the author's favourites, as well as churches that are felt to incorporate all periods of architecture. In addition the list includes a great many churches that are considered 'different' for one reason or another, and some modern ones. As far as possible the list tries to exclude churches that have already been mentioned in the book, but some are so magnificent that you may find – if you have read the book – that they crop up several times. All the churches listed here are considered well worth making a detour to visit.

Abbreviations

C	churchyard/setting
D	doors/porches/entrances
F	font
G	glass/windows
M	monuments (memorials)
P	pulpit
R	roof
RC	Roman Catholic
S	screen/s
W	woodwork/carving
WP	wallpaintings
CCT	Churches Conservation Trust
OCT	Open Churches Trust

Bedfordshire

Bedford: St Paul: P, R, S.
Chalgrave: All Saints: M, WP.
Cockayne Hatley: St John: G, W.
Dunstable: St Peter: G, S.
Eaton Bray: St Mary: D, F, M, S.
Elstow: St Mary and St Helen: F, M.
Felmersham: St Mary: S.
Leighton Buzzard: All Saints: D, F, S, W.
Little Barford: St Denys: F, M (CCT).
Lower Gravenhurst: St Mary: M, S, R (CCT).
Luton: St Mary: S, M, W.
Marston Moretaine: St Mary: G, S, WP.
Milton Bryan: St Peter: G, M.
Odell: All Saints: P, W.
Old Warden: St Leonard: G, W.
Pottesgrove: St Mary: G, S, R (CCT).
Turvey: All Saints: M, R, W.
Wymington: St Lawrence: G, M, W.

Berkshire

Aldermaston: St Mary: M, P, WP.
Aldworth: St Mary: C, M.
Avington: St Mark and St Luke: F.
Bisham: All Saints: M.
East Shefford: St Thomas: G, M, WP (CCT).
Hamstead Marshall: St Mary: P, W.
Lambourn: St Michael: F, G, M.
Langley Marish: St Mary: M, S, W.
Lower Basildon: St Bartholomew: C, F, M (CCT) (OCT).
Newbury: St Nicholas: G.
Reading: St Mary the Virgin: F, S (OCT).
Shottesbrooke: St John Baptist: M.
Sonning: St Andrew: M.
Tidmarsh: St Laurence: D, M.
Warfield: St Michael: S, M.
Wickham: St Swithun: C.
Windsor Castle: St George's Chapel: D, S, W.

Buckinghamshire

Bledlow: Holy Trinity: G, F, WP (OCT).
Broughton: St Lawrence: G, M, WP (CCT).
Chenies: St Michael: M.
Chicheley: St Laurence: M, S.
Clifton Reynes: St Mary the Virgin: F, M.
Edlesborough: St Mary: P, S, G, R, W (CCT).
Gayhurst: St Peter: W, M.
Haddenham: St Mary: F, W.
Hillesden: All Saints: D, G, M, R, S, W.
Ivinghoe: St Mary: D, M , R, W.
Little Kimble: All Saints: WP.
Little Missenden: St John Baptist: F, WP.
Milton Keynes: Christ the Cornerstone: F, G.
North Marston: St Mary: R, W.
Penn: Holy Trinity: C, D, M, P, R, WP.
Pitstone: St Mary: C, W.
Quainton: Holy Cross and St Mary: C, M.
Stewkley: St Michael: D, P.
Stoke Poges: St Giles: C, G, M, R.
Thornton: St Michael and All Angels: M, W (CCT).
West Wycombe: St Lawrence: C, F, M, R, W.
Wing: All Saints: D, F, G, R, M, S.

Cambridgeshire and Huntingdon district

Babraham: St Peter: G, M.
Balsham: Holy Trinity: M, S, W.
Burwell: St Mary: G, M, R, W.
Bottisham: Holy Trinity: M, S.
Cambridge: All Saints: S, W (CCT); St Botolph: F, S; St Mary the
   Great: R, W; Holy Sepulchre: G.
Duxford St John: M, W, WP (CCT).
Hildersham: Holy Trinity: M.
Ickleton: St Mary: WP.
Isleham: St Andrew: M.
March: St Wendreda: R.
Parson Drove: St John Baptist: P, W (CCT).
Peakirk: St Pega's: WP.
Swaffham Prior: St Mary: G.
Trumpington: St Mary and St Michael: G, M.

Wisbech: St Peter and St Paul: D, G, M.

Huntingdon district

Alconbury: St Peter and St Paul: R.
Barnack: St John: F.
Castor: St Kyneburgha: R, WP.
Conington: All Saints: M (CCT).
Leighton Bromswold: St Mary: W.
Little Gidding: St John: G, W.
Offord D'Arcy: St Peter: M, W (CCT).
Ramsey: St Thomas: G, R.
St Ives: All Saints: F, S, W.
Thorney: St Mary and St Botolph: G.
Yaxley: St Peter: M, P, S, W, WP.

Cheshire

Acton: St Mary: S, M.
Astbury: St Mary: D, P, S.
Baddiley: St Michael: D, P, M, W.
Barthomley: St Bertoline: C, M.
Birtles: St Catherine: G.
Bunbury: St Boniface: D, M. S.
Chester: St John Baptist: G, M, R (OCT).
Congleton: St Peter: G, P, W.
Eccleston: St Mary the Virgin: G, W.
Great Budworth: St Mary and All Saints: C, F, R, W.
Lower Peover: St Oswald: C, S, P, M, R.
Macclesfield: Christ Church: G, M (CCT); St Michael: G, M.
Malpas: St Oswald: R, S, W, M.
Marton: St James and St Paul: P, R.
Mobberley: St Wilfrid: R, S, WP.
Mottram: St Michael and All Angels: C, M, R (OCT).
Nantwich: St Mary: R, M, W.
Prestbury: St Peter: C, F, G, P (OCT).
Shotwick: St Michael: G, P, W.
Warrington: St Elphin: G, M.

Cornwall

Altarnun: St Nonna: F, W.
Blisland: SS Proteus and Hyacinth: C, F, R, S.
Bodmin: St Petroc: F, R, S, M (see Jenkins) (OCT).
Breage: St Breaca: WP.
Come-to-Good: Quaker Meeting House: R, W.
Golant: St Sampson: G, R, W.
Gunwalloe: St Winwaloe: C, R.
Kilkhampton: St James: D, G, M, W.
Laneast: SS Sidwell and Gulval: G, R, S, W.
Launcells: St Swithin: C, F, P, R, W.
Launceston: St Mary: P, R, M.
Madron: St Maddern: C, R, M, W.
Morwenstow: St John Baptist: C, F, R, W, WP.
Mullion: St Melina: D, S, W.
Mylor: St Mylor: C, P, S.
Probus: St Probus and St Grace: M, W.
St Buryan: St Buryan: S.
St Germans: St Germanus: G, S, M.
St Just-in-Penwith: WP.
St Just-in-Roseland: C.
St Mawgan-in-Pydar: C, F, S, W.
St Neot: G.
St Winnow: C, G, P, S, W.
Tintagel: St Materiana: C.
Trebetherick: St Enodoc: C, F (OCT).
Tremaine: St Winwalloe: C, D, F.

Cumbria

Appleby: St Lawrence: S, W, M.
Armathwaite: Chapel of Christ and St Mary: C, R (OCT).
Barton: St Michael: C, R.
Beckermet: St Bridget: C.
Beetham: St Michael: G, S, W (OCT).
Bolton: All Saints: F, S.
Bridekirk: St Bridget: F.
Brougham: St Ninian: P, S, W (CCT); St Wilfrid: W.
Cartmel: St Mary and St Michael: G, S, W.
Crosthwaite: St Kentigern: F, M.
Eskdale: St Catherine: C, G.

Greystoke: St Andrew: G, W.
Kendal: Holy Trinity: M.
Kirkby Lonsdale: St Mary: P, S, W.
Lanercost Priory: C, G.
Lowther: St Michael: C, M.
Ravenstonedale: St Oswald: W.
St Bees: St Mary and St Bega: D, S.
Torpenhow: St Michael: C, D, R.
Waberthwaite: St John: C, P.
Wasdale Head: St Olaf: C, W.
Whitehaven: St James: D, F, R (OCT).
Wreay: St Mary: G, P, W.

Derbyshire

Ashbourne: St Oswald: C, G, M.
Ashover: All Saints: F, M.
Ault Hucknall: St John: D, M (OCT).
Bakewell: All Saints: M, S, W.
Chesterfield: St Mary and All Saints: F, M, P, S.
Dale Abbey: P, W, WP (OCT).
Derby: St Mary (RC): G.
Edensor: St Peter: M.
Eyam: St Lawrence: S, WP.
Foremark: St Saviour: P, M, S, W.
Kedleston: All Saints: M, W (CCT).
Melbourne: St Michael and St Mary: D, WP.
Morley: St Matthew: G, M.
Norbury: St Mary and St Barlock: C, G, M.
Repton: St Wynstan: D, R, M.
Sandiacre: St Giles: C, G, M.
Sawley: All Saints: M, S.
Steetley: All Saints: D, M, R.
Tideswell: St John Baptist: M, W.
Whitwell: St Lawrence: F, W.
Wirksworth: St Mary: C, M.
Youlgreave: All Saints: G, F, M.

Devon

Ashton: St John Baptist, Upper Ashton: C, S, P, M, R, W.
Atherington: St Mary: G, S, M, R, W.
Babbacombe: All Saints: F, G, P.
Branscombe: St Winifred: C, M, P, S, W, WP.
Bovey Tracey: St Thomas: F, M, R, S.
Brentor: St Michael-of-the-Rock: C, M.
Colyton: St Andrew: M, S.
Crediton: Holy Cross: F, G, M, R, S.
Cullompton: St Andrew: R, S.
Chittlehampton: St Hieritha: C, D, M, P, R.
Chulmleigh: St Mary: R, S.
Dartmouth: St Saviour: D, M, P, S, W.
Exeter: St Martin: F, G, M, W (CCT); St Mary Steps: F, S, W.
Harberton: St Andrew: C, D, F, P, S.
Hartland: St Nectan: F, M, S.
Marwood: St Michael: M, R, S, W.
Molland: St Mary the Virgin: C, P, R, M.
Morebath: St George: C, M, R.
Ottery St Mary: St Mary: F, G, R, M, W.
Paignton: St John: P, S.
Parracombe: St Petroc: S, M, W (CCT).
Pilton: St Mary: F, P, S, M.
Swimbridge: St James: P, R, S, W.
Torbryan: Holy Trinity: D, G, R, S, W (CCT).
Totnes: St Mary: D, F, M, R, S.
Witheridge: St John Baptist: F, P, G.

Dorset

Bere Regis: St John Baptist: F, R, W.
Blandford Forum: St Peter and St Paul: P, W (OCT).
Bothenhampton: Holy Trinity: F, P.
Bournemouth: St Stephen: S, W, WP.
Cattistock: SS Peter and Paul: G.
Cerne Abbas: St Mary: P, S, WP.
Chalbury: All Saints: P, W.
Charlton Marshall: St Mary: W.
Christchurch Priory: S, M, R.
Loders: St Mary Magdalene: C, F, G, M.
Milton Abbas: Milton Abbey: C, G, M, R, S, W.

Moreton: St Nicholas: G.
Puddletown: St Mary: F, M, R.
Sherborne: Abbey Church of St Mary: M, R, W.
Studland: St Nicholas: F, M, R.
Tarrant Crawford: St Mary: WP, W.
Trent: St Andrew: R, M, S.
Wareham: St Martin: M, WP.
Whitcombe: (dedication unknown): P, S, M, WP (CCT).
Wimborne Minster: St Cuthburga: F, G, M, W.
Wimborne St Giles: St Giles: R, S, M.
Winterborne Tomson: St Andrew: R, W (CCT).
Worth Matravers: St Adhelm: C.

Durham and Tyne & Wear

Barnard Castle: St Mary: G, M (OCT).
Brancepeth: St Brandon: C, D, R, S, W, M.
Chester-le-Street: St Mary and St Cuthbert: F, M, W (OCT).
Darlington: St Cuthbert: M, R.
Durham City: St Mary-le-Bow: S, W.
Escomb: St John: C, D, G, WP.
Gibside Chapel: P, R, W.
Hartlepool: St Hilda: C, M (OCT).
Jarrow: St Paul: G, W.
Lanchester: All Saints: G, W.
Monkwearmouth: St Peter with St Cuthbert: G, M.
Newburn: St Michael and All Angels: W, WP (OCT).
Newcastle upon Tyne: St John: F, G, P; St John Baptist: G.
Pittington: St Lawrence: F, G, M, WP.
Roker: St Andrew: G, M, R, W.
Seaham: St Mary: C, G.
Sedgefield: St Edmund: S, M, W (OCT).
Staindrop: St Mary: D, M.
Stanhope: St Thomas: G, W.
Sunderland: Holy Trinity: F, S, M, W (CCT).

Essex

Belchamp Walter: St Mary the Virgin: F, M, W.
Blackmore: St Laurence: D, M.
Bocking: St Mary: S.

Bradwell-juxta-Coggeshall: Holy Trinity: D, M, S, WP.
Bradwell-on-Sea: St Peter on the Wall: C.
Castle Hedingham: St Nicholas: M, R, S, W.
Chickney: St Mary: C (CCT).
Chignall Smealy: St Nicholas: F, S, P.
Clavering: SS Mary and Clement: C, F, G, M, R, S.
Colchester: St Leonard at the Hythe: G, R.
Copford: St Michael: F, WP.
Dedham: St Mary: D, F, M.
East Horndon: All Saints: M (CCT).
Epping: St John Baptist: P, S.
Finchingfield: St John: C, S, M.
Great Bardfield: St Mary: S, W.
Great Bromley: St George: D, G, M, R.
Great Warley: St Mary: F, R, S, W.
Greensted: St Andrew: G, W.
Hadstock: St Botolph: D, S, W.
Ingatestone: St Edmund and St Mary: M.
Ingrave: St Nicholas: F, P, M.
Layer Marney: St Mary: M, S.
Radwinter: St Mary: D.
Rivenhall: St Mary: G.
Saffron Walden: St Mary: C, M.
St Osyth: SS Peter and Paul: D, R, M.
Stebbing: St Mary: S.
Thaxted: St John: G, R, W.
Waltham Abbey: Holy Cross: F, M, P, S.
Wendens Ambo: St Mary: P, S.

Gloucestershire and Bristol

Baunton: St Mary Magdalene: D, F, WP.
Berkeley: St Mary: M, S, WP (OCT).
Bibury: St Mary: C, G, M.
Bristol: The New Room (Chapel): P, W; St John Baptist: C, G, R, M
    (CCT); St Mary Redcliffe: D, G, M, R, S, W.
Chedworth: St Andrew: C, G, P.
Chipping Campden: St James: M.
Cirencester: St John Baptist: D, G, M, P, R, WP.
Daglingworth: Holy Rood: C, M.
Deerhurst; St Mary: C, F, G, M.

Duntisbourne Rouse: St Michael: C, F, M, P, WP.
Dymock: St Mary: C, G, M, R.
Elkstone: St John: C, F, R.
Fairford: St Mary: C, D, G, M, R, S, W.
Hailes: (dedication unknown): C, S, W, WP.
Highnam: Holy Innocents: G, M, WP (OCT).
Kempley: St Edward: W; St Mary: D, WP.
Kempsford: St Mary: C, S, M, W.
Leonard Stanley: St Leonard: C, D, R.
North Cerney: All Saints: G, S, R.
Northleach: SS Peter and Paul: C, D, G, P, M, R, S.
Oddington: St Nicholas: C, P, W, WP.
Painswick: St Mary: C, R.
Rendcomb: St Peter: F, G.
Sapperton: St Kenelm: C, M, W.
Sevenhampton: St Andrew: F, M.
Standish: St Nicholas: C, M, P, R, W.
Tetbury: St Mary: R, W.
Tewkesbury: Abbey Church of St Mary: D, G, M, R, W, WP.
Upleadon: St Mary: D, R, W.

Hampshire and the Isle of Wight

Abbotts Ann: St Mary: F, P, W.
Avington: St Mary the Virgin: P, W M.
Boarhunt: St Nicholas: P, W.
Boldre: St John: G, P, M, R.
Breamore: St Mary: D, G.
Burghclere: Sandham Memorial Chapel: WP.
Corhampton: (dedication unknown): F, WP.
Crondall: All Saints: F, R.
Damerham: St George: D, R, W.
Dummer: All Saints: M, P, W.
East Meon: All Saints: F, P.
East Wellow: St Margaret: W, WP.
Ellingham: St Mary: P, S, W.
Freefolk: St Nicholas: F, G, M, W (CCT).
Hambledon: SS Peter and Paul: D, R.
Headbourne Worthy: St Swithun: C.
Minstead: All Saints: C, F, P, W (OCT).
Portchester: St Mary: C, F.

Romsey: Abbey of St Mary and St Ethelflaeda: M, WP.
Selborne: St Mary: C.
Silchester: St Mary: C, P, S.
Stoke Charity: St Mary and St Michael: C, M.
Titchfield: St Peter: M.
Winchester: St Cross: G, R.

Isle of Wight

Brading: St Mary: M, W.
Carisbrooke: St Mary: M.
Godshill: All Saints: C, M, WP.
Shalfleet: St Michael: D, R, W.
Shorwell: St Peter: P, M, W, WP.
Whippingham: St Mildred: M, S.
Yarmouth: St James: M.

Herefordshire

Abbey Dore: Holy Trinity and St Mary: C, R, S.
Bacton: St Faith: M, R, W.
Bosbury: Holy Trinity: C, F, M, P, S, W.
Brinsop: St George: D, G, S.
Brockhampton-by-Ross: All Saints: C, G, R.
Castle Frome: St Michael: F, G, M.
Clodock: St Clodock: C, M, P, W.
Dilwyn: St Mary the Virgin: F, S, M.
Eardisley: St Mary Magdalene: F.
Fownhope: St Mary: G, M.
Hereford: All Saints: R, W, WP; St Peter: R, W.
Hoarwithy: St Catherine: C, M, R.
Kilpeck: SS Mary and David: C, D, F.
Ledbury: St Michael and All Angels: C, F, G, M.
Leominster: Priory Church of SS Peter and Paul: C, G.
Madley: Church of the Nativity of the Virgin: G, M, W.
Monnington on Wye: St Mary: S, W.
Much Marcle: St Bartholomew: C, M.
Pembridge: St Mary: C, F, G, M.
Richards Castle: St Bartholomew: C, G, W (CCT).
St Margarets: St Margaret: C, S.
Sellack: St Tysilio: G, P, M.
Shobdon: St John: G, M, P, W.

Hertfordshire

Anstey: St George: F, W.
Ardeley: St Lawrence: M, R.
Ashwell St Mary: D, G, P, S, W.
Ayot St Lawrence: (New St Lawrence): D, W.
Bengeo: St Leonard: WP.
Bishop's Stortford: St Michael: R, S, W.
Braughing: St Mary: D, M.
Broxbourne: St Augustine: C, D, M, R.
Flamstead: St Leonard: P, R, WP.
Hatfield: St Etheldreda: F, M, S.
Hitchin: St Mary: M, R, S.
Kimpton: SS Peter and Paul: S, W.
Knebworth: St Mary and St Thomas: F, M, W.
Little Hadham: St Cecilia: D, P, S.
Much Hadham: St Andrew: R, S, M.
Oxhey Chapel: (dedication unknown): F, M, W.
Ridge: St Margaret: G, R, M, P, WP.
St Paul's Walden: All Saints: G, S.
South Mimms: St Giles: G, M.
Stanstead Abbots: St James: F, M, P, R, W (CCT).
Ware: St Mary: F, M, R, W.
Watford: Holy Rood (RC): R, S.

Kent

Adisham: Holy Innocents: F.
Aldington: St Martin: S, W.
Ash-next-Sandwich: SS Peter and Paul: M.
Badlesmere: St Leonard: R, W.
Barfrestone: St Nicholas: D, G, W, WP.
Boughton Aluph: All Saints: C, G, WP.
Braybourne: St Mary: G, M.
Brook: St Mary: P, WP.
Brookland: St Augustine: F, P, W, WP.
Burham: St Mary: F (CCT).
Capel: St Thomas Becket: WP (CCT).
Chilham: St Mary: M.
Chillenden: All Saints: P.
Cranbrook: St Dunstan: G.
Elham: St Mary: W.

Fairfield: St Thomas à Becket: C, P, W.
Hythe: St Leonard: C, G.
Ivychurch: St George: D, G, S, W.
Kingsdown: St Catherine: G, W (CCT).
Minster in Thanet: St Mary: M, R, W.
Old Romney: St Clement: C, M, W.
Patrixbourne: St Mary: D, G.
Sandwich: St Clement: D, F: St Peter: R, M (CCT).
Smarden: St Michael: R.
Stelling: St Mary: P, W.
Stone: St Mary: M, WP.
Tudeley: All Saints: G.
Tunbridge Wells: King Charles the Martyr: R, W.

Lancashire, Greater Manchester and Merseyside

Ashton under Lyne: St Michael: G, P, R, W (OCT).
Becconsall: All Saints (CCT).
Billinge: St Aidan: R, M.
Blackburn: Holy Trinity: R (CCT).
Bolton: All Souls: R, W (CCT).
Eccles: St Mary: R.
Great Mitton: All Hallows: P, R, S, M.
Halsall: St Cuthbert: M, W.
Lancaster: St John the Evangelist (CCT); St Mary: P, W.
Liverpool: St Agnes: F; St John, Tue Brook: S, G, R, S, WP.
Manchester: Holy Name of Jesus (RC): R, S; St Ann: W (OCT).
Melling: St Wilfrid: G, M (OCT).
Middleton: St Leonard: G, M (OCT).
Old Langho: St Leonard: G, R, W (CCT).
Ormskirk: SS Peter and Paul: F, S, M.
Pendlebury: St Augustine: G, S.
Pilling: St John Baptist: F, P, W.
Poulton-le-Fylde: St Chad: M, P, S.
Rochdale: St Chad: M, W; St Mary: S, W.
Rufford: St Mary: M.
St Anne's-on-Sea: St Anne: G, P (OCT).
Sefton: St Helen: P, S, P, W.
Slaidburn: St Andrew: S, W.
Southport: St Cuthbert: M.
Standish: St Wilfrid: P, M, W.

Stidd: St Saviour: D, P, S.
Stockport: St George: G, W.
Tarleton: St Mary: W (CCT).
Tunstall: St John Baptist: G (OCT).
Warburton: St Werburgh: W, M.
Warton: St Oswald: C, M (OCT).
Whalley: St Mary: D, W.
Woodplumpton: St Anne: C, M (OCT).

Leicestershire

Beeby: All Saints: F, S, W (CCT).
Bottesford: St Mary the Virgin: M.
Breedon on the hill: St Mary and St Hardulph: F, M, W.
Croxton Kerrial: St John Baptist: W.
Edmondthorpe: St Michael and all Angels: M (CCT).
Gaddesby: St Luke: M.
Gaulby: St Peter: F, G (OCT).
Hallaton: St Michael: D, G.
King's Norton: St John: P, W (OCT).
Leicester: St Margaret of Antioch: M (OCT); St Mary de Castro: C, R
    (OCT).
Lockington: St Nicholas: S, W.
Lubenham: All Saints: C, P, W.
Melton Mowbray: St Mary: D, G, M.
North Kilworth: All Saints: M.
Noseley: St Mary: F, G W.
Ratby: SS Philip and James: G, M (OCT).
Staunton Harold: Holy Trinity: P, S, R, W.
Stoke Golding: St Margaret: F, G.
Withcote Chapel: C, G (CCT).

Lincolnshire

Addlethorpe: St Nicholas: D, G, R, S (OCT).
Bag Enderby: St Margaret: C, F (OCT).
Barnetby-le-Wold: St Mary: C, W (CCT).
Barton-upon-Humber: St Mary: M (OCT); St Peter: D.
Boston: St Botolph: C, D, P, W (OCT).
Brant Broughton: D, R (OCT).
Brumby: St Hugh (Scunthorpe): R (OCT).

Caistor: SS Peter and Paul: C, D, M (OCT).
Coates-by-Stow: St Edith: C, S, P, M (OCT).
Crowland: St Guthlac's Abbey: F, M (OCT).
Gainsborough: All Saints: C, F, R (OCT).
Grantham: St Wulfram: R, M, S (OCT).
Heckington: St Andrew: D, F, M (OCT).
Kirkstead: St Leonard: C, D, M, S.
Lincoln: All Saints: G (OCT); St John Baptist: G (OCT).
Louth: St James: C, R (OCT).
Old Leake: St Mary: M, P.
Snarford: St Lawrence: F, M (CCT).
Stamford: All Saints: M (OCT); St Mary: G, R, S, W (OCT).
Stow: St Mary: F, M, R (OCT).
Stragglethorpe: St Michael: C, P, W.
Tattershall: Holy Trinity: G, P, M, S (OCT).
Walesby: All Saints: C, S, G (OCT).
Whaplode: St Mary: P, M (OCT).

London

North of the River

All Saints, Margaret Street: S, P, R, WP.
All Saints, Poplar: D, P (OCT).
Barking: St Margaret: S, M, W.
Chelsea: Holy Trinity, Sloane Street: G, P, F (OCT).
Clerkenwell: St James: M.
Gospel Oak: St Martin: P, R.
Hampstead: St John: C, W.
Hampstead Garden Suburb: St Jude: G, R, S, WP.
Harringay: St Paul: D, G.
Harrow-on-the-Hill: St Mary: C, G, P.
Hoxton: St John Baptist: P, R (OCT).
Kensington: St Augustine: R; St Cuthbert: G, R.
Kilburn: St Augustine: G, WP.
Limehouse: St Anne: D, G, R.
Paddington: St Mary Magdalene: G, R.
Pimlico: St Barnabas: P, S (OCT).
Poplar: All Saints: P (OCT).
Shoreditch: St Leonard: F, M, W (OCT).
Spitalfields: Christ Church: D, R.
St Cyprian, Clarence Gate: F, S.

St James-the-Less, Vauxhall Bridge Road: F, G, WP (OCT).
St Martin-in-the-Fields, Trafalgar Square: D, R, W.
St Mary-le-Strand, WC2: D, R, W.
St Paul, Covent Garden: R, W.
Westminster: St Margaret: G.
Willesden: St Mary: F.

South of the River

Camberwell: St Giles: M.
Charlton: St Luke: F, M.
Deptford: St Paul: G, R, W (OCT).
Dulwich: St Barnabas: G.
Greenwich: St Alfege: R, W (OCT).
Kew Green: St Anne: G, M, W.
Lambeth: St Mary: M.
North Brixton: Christ Church: P.
Peckham: St John: G.
Petersham: St Peter: C, P, M, W.
Tooting Graveney: All Saints: F, P, W.
Vauxhall: St Peter: G, S.
West Dulwich: All Saints: S.

City Churches

All Hallows by the Tower: F, G, M, P, W.
St Bartholomew the Great, Smithfield: G, M.
St Bride, Fleet St: G, S, R, W.
St Clement, Eastcheap: F, W.
St Helen, Bishopsgate: D, M.
St John Baptist, Hoxton: R (OCT).
St Margaret Lothbury: P, S, W.
St Margaret Pattens: P, W.
St Martin, Ludgate Hill: D, P, S, W.
St Mary Aldermary: F, R, W.
St Mary-le-Bow: G, R, W.
St Mary Woolnoth: P, R, M, W.
St Stephen Walbrook: F, P, R, W.
St Vedast-alias-Foster: F, R.
Temple Church: G, M.

Greater London

Cranford: St Dunstan: C, F, G.
Ealing: St Peter: G, R.
Enfield: St Andrew: M.
Harefield: St Mary: C, P, M, R.
Harlington: St Paul: D, F.
Harmondsworth: St Mary: D.
Hayes: St Mary: R, WP.
Ickenham: St Giles: D, F, M, R.
Northolt: St Mary: F, M, R.
Petersham: St Peter: P, W.
Ruislip: St Martin: D, P, R, W.
Stanmore: St Lawrence: M, R, W.
Twickenham: St Mary: C, F, M, P.
Whitchurch: St Lawrence, Little Stanmore: M, W.

Norfolk

Attleborough: St Mary: P, S, WP.
Beeston-next-Mileham: St Mary: P, R, S, W.
Binham: Priory of St Mary: C, S, W.
Blakeney: St Nicholas: C, G, R.
Burnham Deepdale: St Mary: F, G.
Burnham Norton: St Margaret: C, F, P, S, WP.
Castle Acre: St James: C, P, S.
Cawston: St Agnes: D, P, R, S, W.
Cley-next-the-Sea: St Margaret: C, D, G, P, W.
East Dereham: St Nicholas: F, G, S (OCT).
East Harling: St Peter and St Paul: G, M (OCT).
Erpingham: St Mary: G, M, W (OCT).
Hales: St Margaret: C, F, P, S (CCT).
Houghton-on-the Hill: St Mary: WP.
Ingham: Holy Trinity: D, R, M.
King's Lynn: St Margaret: M, S, W.
Little Snoring: St Andrew: C, F.
North Elmham: St Mary: G, S, W.
Norwich: St Andrew: G, M (OCT); St George Tombland: M, W
    (OCT); St Giles: M, R (OCT); St John Maddermarket: D, G, M, R,
    S, W (CCT); St Peter Mancroft: F, G, R, M, W.
Oxborough: St John: M.
Ranworth: St Helen: S.

Reepham: St Mary: C, D, F, G, M.
Salle: St Peter and St Paul: C, D, F, G, P, R, W.
South Lopham: St Andrew: G, W (OCT).
Tilney: All Saints: C, S.
Trunch: St Botolph: F, R, S, W.
Walpole: St Peter: C, D, F, S, W.
Walsoken: All Saints: F, R, S, W.
Wymondham: St Mary and St Thomas: C, R, S.

Northamptonshire

Ashby St Ledgers: St Leodegarius: F, M, P, S, W, WP (OCT).
Brigstock: St Andrew: C, M.
Brixworth: All Saints: C, S.
Burton Latimer: St Mary the Virgin: M, WP (OCT).
Croughton: All Saints: M, WP.
Daventry: Holy Cross: P, W (OCT).
Earls Barton: All Saints: D, S, T.
Fotheringay: St Mary and All Saints: C, F, P, R.
Geddington: St Mary Magdalene: G, S (OCT).
Great Brington: St Mary: M, W.
Harrington: SS Peter and Paul: M, S.
Higham Ferrers: St Mary: D, S, M, W.
Holdenby: All Saints: M, S, W (CCT).
Little Billing: All Saints: F.
Lowick: St Peter: G, M.
Middleton Cheney: All Saints: G.
Northampton: Holy Sepulchre: G, R, S; St Matthew: G, D, R (OCT);
    St Peter: F (CCT).
Passenham: St Guthlac: R, W, WP.
Raunds: St Mary: WP.
Rothwell: Holy Trinity: C.
Stanford on Avon: St Nicholas: G, M, W.
Warkton: St Edmund: M.
Wellingborough: All Hallows: G, R, S, W (OCT); St Mary: F, S.

Northumberland

Alnwick: St Michael: G, M.
Bamburgh: St Aidan: C, G, M.
Bellingham: St Cuthbert: R.
Berwick-upon-Tweed: Holy Trinity: W (OCT).
Blanchland: St Mary: C, G, M.
Brinkburn Priory: SS Peter and Paul: C, D, R.
Bywell: St Peter: G.
Chillingham: St Peter: M, P, R.
Corbridge: St Andrew: G.
Haltwhistle: Holy Cross: F, G (OCT).
Hexham: Priory Church of St Andrew: P, M, S, R, W.
Holy Island: St Mary: C.
Kirknewton: St Gregory: C, R, M.
Norham: St Cuthbert: G, M, W.
Ovingham: St Mary: G.
Warkworth: St Lawrence: R, M.

Nottinghamshire

Blidworth: St Mary: C, W.
Blyth: St Mary and St Martin: C, F, S, WP.
Clifton: St Mary: C, M.
Clumber: St Mary: R, W.
Coddington: All Saints: G.
East Markham: St John Baptist: G, M.
Egmanton: St Mary: D, F, S.
Elston Chapel: D, WP (CCT).
Hawton: All Saints: G.
Holme: St Giles: G, M, W.
Kingston on Soar: St Wilfrid: M.
Newark: St Mary: S, W.
Nottingham: St Mary: D, M.
Ossington: Holy Rood: M.
Ratcliffe on Soar: Holy Trinity: M.
Saundby St Martin: G, M (CCT).
Sibthorpe: St Peter: G, M, W.
Strelley: All Saints: G, M, S.
Willoughby-on-the-Wolds: St Mary and All Saints: M.
Worksop: St Mary and St Cuthbert: D, R.
Wysall: Holy Trinity: M, R, S, W.

Oxfordshire

Abingdon: St Helen: C, R, W (OCT).
Adderbury: St Mary: S, R.
Bloxham: St Mary: G, M, WP.
Broughton: St Mary: F, M, WP.
Burford: St John: C, G, M.
Chalgrove: St Mary: R, M, WP (OCT).
Childrey: St Mary: G, M.
Chislehampton: St Katherine: P, W (CCT).
Dorchester: Abbey of St Peter and St Paul: G, M.
Ewelme: St Mary: C, M, R, S.
Faringdon: All Saints: C, D, M.
Freeland: St Mary: G, S, WP.
Iffley: St Mary: D, G, W.
Kelmscott: St George: G, WP.
Kidlington: St Mary: G, W, WP (OCT).
Minster Lovell: St Kenelm: C, M.
North Leigh: St Mary: M, S, WP.
North Stoke: St Mary: F, P, W, WP.
Oxford: St Giles: F, M (OCT); St Mary the Virgin: G, R, W.
Rycote: St Michael: D, P, R, WP.
Shrivenham: St Andrew: P, M, S, W.
South Newington: St Peter ad Vincula: G, WP (OCT).
Stanton Harcourt: St Michael: M, S.
Swinbrook: St Mary: M.
Uffington: St Mary: D, W.
Wheatfield: St Andrew: C, P, M, W.
Widford: St Oswald: C, P, W, WP.
Yarnton: St Bartholomew: G, S, M.

Rutland

Barrowden: St Peter: P, M.
Brooke: St Peter: M, S, W.
Burley: Holy Cross: M (CCT).
Exton: SS Peter and Paul: M.
Ketton: St Mary: D, W.
Little Casterton: All Saints: M, WP.
Lyddington: St Andrew: W, WP.
North Luffenham: St John: G.
Oakham: All Saints: W.

Stoke Dry: St Andrew: M, W.
Teigh: Holy Trinity: F, P, R, W.
Tickencote: SS Peter and Paul: W.

Shropshire

Acton Burnell: St Mary: F, P, M.
Bromfield: St Mary: R, P, M, S.
Burford: St Mary: M, R.
Claverley: All Saints: F, P, M, WP.
Cound: St Peter: F, G, M, P, S.
Heath Chapel (no dedication): C, D, P, W.
Kinlet: St John Baptist: G, M.
Langley Chapel (no dedication): R, W.
Llanyblodwel: St Michael: C, F, S, M.
Ludlow: St Laurence: D, G, M, W.
Melverley: St Peter: C, P, W.
Minsterley: Holy Trinity: P, W.
Pitchford: St Michael: M, P, W.
Quatt: St Andrew: F, P, S, M.
Selattyn: St Mary: F, P, R (OCT).
Shrewsbury: Holy Cross (Abbey): M; St Chad: C, D, M; St Mary the
    Virgin: D, F, G, M, R, W (CCT).
Stokesay: St John Baptist: C, M, W.
Stottesdon: St Mary: F, G, P, S.
Tong: St Bartholomew: F, G, S, M.
Worfield: St Peter: D, G, M.
Wroxeter: St Andrew: M, P, W (CCT).

Somerset

Axbridge: St John: S, M, R.
Banwell: St Andrew: D, P, S.
Bath: Abbey church: M, R.
Brympton D'Evercy: St Andrew: C, G, M, S.
Crewkerne: St Bartholomew: R, S.
Croscombe: St Mary: P, S, W.
Crowcombe: Holy Ghost: F, S, W.
Culbone: St Culbone: C, F, R, W.
Dunster: St George: S.
Glastonbury: St John: G, R.

Holcombe: St Andrew: C, P, W (CCT).
Ilminster: St Mary: M, W (OCT).
Isle Abbotts: St Mary: D, F, S, W.
Martock: All Saints: D, R.
Mells: St Andrew: C, M.
Muchelney: SS Peter and Paul: R.
Selworthy: All Saints: C, D, R.
Shepton Mallett: SS Peter and Paul: P, R.
Somerton: St Michael: R, W.
Stogumber: St Mary: M, P, W.
Stogursey: St Andrew: M, S, W.
Swell: St Catherine: C, F, P, W.
Taunton: St Mary Magdalene: D, R.
Wells: St Cuthbert: R.
Westonzoyland: St Mary: R.

Staffordshire

Blore Ray: St Bartholomew: C, S, M, W (OCT).
Bobbington: Holy Cross: M (OCT).
Brewood: St Mary the Virgin and St Chad: F, M (OCT).
Broughton: St Peter: G, W.
Cheadle: St Giles (RC): C, G, P, S.
Clifton Campville: St Andrew: M.
Elford: St Peter: D, M.
Forton: All Saints: M.
Gnosall: St Lawrence: C, G (OCT).
Hamstall Ridware: St Michael: C, S, G, M.
Hoar Cross: Holy Angels: R, S, M (OCT).
Ingestre: St Mary: P, R, M, W.
Kinver: St Peter: M, P (OCT).
Mavesyn Ridware: St Nicholas: M.
Penkridge: St Michael: M, S, W.
Stafford: St Mary: G, R, W (OCT).
Tamworth: St Editha: G, R, M.
Tutbury: St Mary: D.

Suffolk

Badley: St Mary: C, M, W (CCT).
Blythburgh: Holy Trinity: C, R, W.
Bramfield: St Andrew: C, M, S.
Dennington: St Mary: D, F, M, P, R, S, W.
Earl Stonham: St Mary: R, W (OCT).
Eye: SS Peter and Paul: R, W.
Framlingham: St Michael: M.
Gipping: St Nicholas: G, W.
Icklingham: All Saints: C, G, R, W (CCT).
Ipswich: St Margaret: D, R; St Mary at Quay: F, R (CCT).
Kedington: SS Peter and Paul: M, P, R, S, W (OCT).
Kersey: St Mary: R W.
Lavenham: SS Peter and Paul: C, D, S.
Long Melford: Holy Trinity: C, G, R.
Mendlesham: St Mary: C, D, W.
Mildenhall: St Mary and St Andrew: G, R, W.
Needham Market: St John: R, W.
Southwold: St Edmund: C, D, R, W.
Stoke-by-Nayland: St Mary: C, D, M.
Thornton Parva: St Mary: G, R (OCT).
Ufford: St Mary: C, F, R, W (OCT).
Wenhaston: St Peter: F, R, WP.
Wingfield: St Andrew: M (OCT).
Woolpit: St Mary: D, R, S.
Yaxley: St Mary: D, S, W.

Surrey

Albury: St Peter and St Paul: G, M, WP (CCT).
Bletchingley: St Mary: M (OCT).
Chaldon: St Peter and St Paul: P, WP.
Charlwood: St Nicholas: S, W, WP.
Chilworth: St Martha: C, D.
Compton: St Nicholas: G, P, R, S.
Dunsfold: St Mary and All Saints: W.
Esher: St George: P, M (CCT).
Gatton: St Andrew: D, G, P, W (OCT).
Hascombe: St Peter: G, R.
Holmbury: St Mary: C, W.
Lingfield: SS Peter and Paul: R, W, M.

Lower Kingswood: St Sophia: D, P, R.
Ockham: All Saints: G, R, M.
Pyrford: St Nicholas: P, R, WP.
Shere: St James: D, F, G, R .
Stoke D'Abernon: St Mary: R, G, P, M.
West Horsley: St Mary: D, G, S, M, WP.

Sussex

Amberley: St Michael: R, WP.
Berwick: St Michael and All Angels: WP.
Bishopstone: St Andrew: C, R .
Bosham: Holy Trinity: C, D, F.
Boxgrove: SS Mary and Blaise: G, M, R.
Brighton: St Michael and All Angels: G, W.
Burton (dedication unknown): F, M, S, W.
Chichester: St John's Chapel: P (CCT).
Clayton: St John: WP.
Coombes (dedication unknown): D, R, WP.
Didling: St Andrew: C, F, P, W.
Hardham: St Botolph: W, WP.
New Shoreham: St Mary: R.
North Stoke (dedication unknown): G, W, WP (CCT).
Old Shoreham: St Nicholas: G, R, S, W.
Playden: St Michael: S, M.
Rotherfield: St Denys: C, G, M, P, R, WP.
Rye: St Mary: C, G.
Sompting: St Mary: R.
South Harting: SS Mary and Gabriel: C, R, M.
Southease (dedication unknown): R, W, WP.
Up Marden: St Michael: C, R, W.
Wadhurst: St Mary: C, M.
Warminghurst: The Holy Sepulchre: M, R, S, W (CCT).
West Chiltington: St Mary: R, WP.
West Grinstead: St George: M, S.
Winchelsea: St Thomas: G, M, WP.
Wisborough Green: St Peter Ad Vincula: C, D, WP.
Worth: St Nicholas: C, F, P.

Warwickshire, Birmingham and West Midlands

Astley: St Mary: M, P, W.

Avon Dassett: St John Baptist: M (CCT).

Berkswell: St John: C, D, M, W.

Binley: St Bartholomew: R.

Birmingham: St Martin, Bull Ring: G, M; Bordesley: St Alban: R, W; Handsworth: St Mary: M; King's Norton: St Nicholas: G, R, M; Sparkbrook: St Agatha: R, W.

Burton Dassett: All Saints: WP.

Castle Bromwich: St Mary and St Margaret: W.

Coughton: St Peter: G, M.

Coventry: Holy Trinity: P, R, W.

Hampton Lucy: St Peter ad Vincula: C, G, W.

Lapworth: St Mary: C, D, R .

Lower Shuckburgh: St John: R, M, W.

Merevale: Our Lady: G, S.

Preston on Stour: St Mary: M.

Solihull: St Alphege: G.

Stratford-upon-Avon: Holy Trinity: G, M, R.

Warwick: St Mary: G, M, R, S.

Whichford: St Michael: G, M.

Wolfhampcote: St Peter: C, S (CCT).

Wootton Wawen: St Peter: C, F, M, P, S.

Wolverhampton: St Peter: M, P, S, W (OCT).

Wiltshire

Alton Barnes: St Mary: F, G, P.

Avebury: St James: F, S.

Bradford-on-Avon: Holy Trinity: G, R, M; St Lawrence: C.

Bromham: St Nicholas: D, G, R, M.

Chippenham: St Andrew: G, W.

Cricklade: St Sampson: C, G, R.

Devizes: St John Baptist: D, F, P, W.

Edington: St Mary, St Katharine and All Saints: F, M, P, R.

Great Chatfield: All Saints: P, M, S.

Inglesham: St John Baptist: C, G, P, S, W, WP (CCT).

Lacock: St Cyriac: M.

Lydiard Tregoze: St Mary: G, M, S, WP.

Malmesbury: The Abbey: D, M, S, W.

Mere: St Michael: G, S (OCT).

Mildenhall: St John: M, P, R.
Oaksey: All Saints: G, WP.
Old Dilton: St Mary: M, W (CCT).
Potterne: St Mary: F, O, W.
Purton: St Mary: D, F, G, P, R, W, WP.
Salisbury: St Thomas: R, M, WP.
Steeple Ashton: St Mary the Virgin: D, G, M, R, W.
Tisbury: St John Baptist: D, M, R.
Urchfont: St Michael: G, R, M.
Wanborough: St Andrew: M.
Wilton: St Mary and St Nicholas: F, G, M, P.

Worcestershire

Besford: St Peter: S, M, W.
Bredon: St Giles: M, W.
Broadway: St Eadburgha: W.
Chaddesley Corbett: St Cassian: F, M.
Croome D'Abitot: St Mary: M (CCT).
Dodford: Holy Trinity and St Mary: R, W.
Elmley Castle: St Mary: C, M.
Evesham: All Saints: C, R.
Great Malvern: The Priory Church: C, G.
Great Witley: St Michael: F, G, M.
Hanbury: St Mary: C, G, M, R.
Holt: St Martin: D, F, G, R.
Little Malvern Priory: St Giles: C, G, M, S, W.
Martley: St Peter: WP.
Pershore: The Abbey: C, G, M.
Ripple: St Mary: W.
Rochford: St Michael: C, D, G.
Rock: St Peter and St Paul: D, F, M.
Shelsley Walsh: St Andrew: C, M, R, S.
Strensham: SS Philip and James: F, M, P, W.
Tenbury Wells: St Michael: G, S.
Worcester: St Swithun: G, M, P, R, W (CCT).

Yorkshire

East Riding

Bainton: St Andrew: F, M, W.
Beverley: The Minster: C, F, G, M, S, W; St Mary: G, R.
Boynton: St Andrew: M, W.
Bridlington: Priory: D, F, G.
Cowlam: St Mary: C, F, M.
Garton on the Wolds: St Michael: G, WP (OCT).
Hedon: St Augustine: F, P.
Howden: Minster of St Peter and St Paul: D, S.
Hull: Holy Trinity: G, R, M.
Lockington: St Mary: P, S, W.
Patrington: St Patrick: R, S, W.
South Dalton: St Mary: M.

North Yorkshire

Allerton Mauleverer: St Martin: R, M.
Bolton Abbey: St Mary and St Cuthbert: C.
Bolton Percy: All Saints: F, G, M, P, R, W.
Cowthorpe: St Michael: F, G (CCT).
Coxwold: St Michael: G, W, M.
Croft: St Peter: M, W.
Filey: St Oswald: D, G.
Hemingbrough: St Mary the Virgin: S, M, W.
Hornby: St Mary: F, S.
Hubberholme: St Michael: C, D, S, W.
Kirk Hammerton: St John Baptist: W.
Kirkdale: St Gregory: D, M.
Knaresborough: St John Baptist: C, M.
Lastingham: St Mary: C.
Masham: St Mary: M.
Pickering: St Peter and St Paul: P, M, WP.
Selby: The Abbey: G, R, W.
Stanwick: St John: C, M (CCT).
Stillingfleet: St Helen: D, G, M.
Studley Royal: St Mary: C, G.
Weaverthorpe: All Saints: C, F.
Wensley: Holy Trinity: D, F, M, P, W.
West Tanfield: St Nicholas: C, G, M.

Whitby: St Mary: C, F, P, W.

York

All Saints, North Street: G, P, R, W.
Holy Trinity, Goodramgate: G, P, W (CCT) (OCT).
St Denys: G, M (OCT).

Yorkshire West and South

Adel: St John Baptist: D.
Birkin: St Mary: F, G, P.
Bramhope: Puritan Chapel: W.
Brigflatts: Friends' Meeting House: D, W.
Campsall: St Mary Magdalene: P, S, M.
Cantley: St Wilfrid: D, M, S.
Doncaster: St George: D, M.
Ecclesfield: St Mary the Virgin: F, R, S, W.
Fishlake: St Cuthbert: D, F.
Halifax: St John the Baptist: G, W.
Harewood: All Saints: C, M (CCT).
Harrogate: St Wilfrid: F, P.
Hatfield: St Lawrence: S, M.
High Bradfield: St Nicholas: C, W.
Ledsham: All Saints: G, M.
Leeds: St John: R, S, W (CCT); St Peter: G, P.
Methley: St Oswald: M, P, R, S.
Rotherham: All Saints: P, S, W; Bridge Chapel of Our Lady: G, W.
Saltaire: United Reformed Church: R, W.
Thornhill: St Michael: G, M.
Tickhill: St Mary the Virgin: F, G, M, S.
Wakefield: Bridge Chapel of St Mary: G.
Womersley: St Martin: G, M.

*   *   *

North Wales

Anglesey and Gwynedd

Beaumaris: St Mary and St Nicholas: M, W.
Llaneilian: St Eilian: R, S.
Llangwyfan: St Cwyfan: C, R.
Tal-y-Llyn: St Mary: R.

Other churches in Gwynedd (Caernarvonshire)

Clynnog-fawr: St Beuno: R, M.
Llangelynin: St Celynin: C, D.
Llanrwst: St Grwst: M, S (OCT).

Clwyd (Denbighshire/Flintshire)

Bodelwyddan: St Margaret: F, G.
Chirk: St Mary: R, W.
Denbigh: St Hilary: S.
Efenechdyd: St Michael: D, F, M.
Gresford: All Saints: S, M, W.
Hanmer: St Chad: C, G, W.
Holt: St Chad: S, R, M.
Holywell: St Winefride (RC): C.
Llandysilio: St Tysilio: M, R (OCT).
Llanrhaeadr: St Dyfnog: G, R, M.
Llanynys: St Saeran: F, M, WP.
Northop: St Eugain and St Peter: M.
Overton: St Mary: F, M, S.
Rug Chapel (no dedication): C, R, W, WP.
Worthenbury: St Deiniol: G, W.
Wrexham: St Giles: M, S (OCT).

Mid Wales

Powys

Llananno: St Anno: F, S, W.
Llanfilo: St Bilo: S, M.
Montgomery: St Nicholas: M, R, S, W.
Old Radnor: St Stephen: S, M.
Patrishow: St Ishow: C, F, S, M, WP.

Pilleth: St Mary: C, F, R.
Presteigne: St Andrew: F, R, M.

Dyfed (Carmarthenshire)

Carmarthen: St Peter: M.
Haverfordwest: St Mary: R, M.
Kidwelly: St Mary: C, M.
Llandeloy: St Teilo: C.
Manordeifi: St David: M.

South-East Wales

Glamorgan

Ewenny: St Michael: F, S, M.
Llancarfan: St Cadoc: F, S.
Llantwit Major: St Illtyd: F, M.
Newton Nottage: St John Baptist: P.
St Donats: St Donat: F, M.

Gwent

Abergavenny: St Mary: F, M, W.
Bettws-Newydd (dedication unknown): F, R, S.
Cwmyoy: St Martin: C, R.
Grosmont: St Nicholas: C, G, S.
Llangwm Uchaf: St Jerome: G, S.
Monmouth: St Mary: G, M.
Skenfrith: St Bridget: G, M, W.

Appendix 3

Useful Contacts

One of your major problems as a church explorer will be access to churches. Just in case you have missed it there is section of the book (Part 5) devoted to this subject. One of the best ways to be sure to gain entry to a church you would like to visit is to find out which diocese it is in and telephone the relevant diocesan office to find the telephone number of the incumbent and main church officials. You will generally find the person on the swithchboard will be able to provide the key names and contact numbers. That is about the most sure method of gaining entry. Rather than doing this before setting out on a church exploring trip it is perfectly possible to do this while 'on the road' with the aid of a mobile phone. However, as this is likely to be more of a last-minute effort you might find yourself talking to an answerphone. For this reason a few days' notice, if you are able to take this approach, is the preferred way of being certain of getting inside all the churches you wish to visit.

About half the Anglican dioceses in England and Wales have tourism officers, and if you make contact with a particular diocesan office it might be useful to obtain the name and contact details of their tourism officer, if they have one, for possible future use. There is also a national Church Tourism Association – see details below.

Telephone numbers of all diocesan offices in England and Wales

England

Bath and Wells: 01749 670777
Birmingham: 0121 4260 400
Blackburn: 01254 54421
Bradford: 01535 650555
Bristol: 0117 9060 100
Canterbury: 01227 459401
Carlisle: 01228 522573

Chelmsford: 01245 294400
Chester: 01244 620444
Chichester: 01273 421021
Coventry: 024 7652 1220
Derby: 01332 388650
Durham: 01388 604515
Ely: 01353 652701
Exeter: 01392 272686
Gloucester: 01452 410022
Guildford: 01483 571826
Hereford: 01432 373300
Leicester: 0116 2487 400
Lichfield: 01543 306030
Lincoln: 01522 529241
Liverpool: 0151 7099 722
London: 020 7932 1100
Manchester: 0161 8339 521
Newcastle: 0191 270 4100
Norwich: 01603 880853
Oxford: 01865 208200
Peterborough: 01733 887000
Portsmouth: 023 9282 5731
Ripon and Leeds: 0113 2487 487
Rochester: 01634 83333
St Albans: 01727 854532
St Edmundsbury and Ipswich: 01473 298500
Salisbury: 01722 411922
Sheffield: 01709 309100
Sodor and Man: 01624 626994
Southwark: 020 7939 9400
Southwell: 01636 817204
Truro: 01872 274351
Wakefield: 01924 371802
Winchester: 01962 844644
Worcester: 01905 20537
York: 01904 699500

Wales

Bangor: 01248 354999
Llandaff: 029 2057 8899
Monmouth: 01633 267490

St Asaph: 01745 582245
St David's: 01267 236145/238527
Swansea and Brecon: 01874 623716

Other useful addresses

Ancient Monuments Society: St Ann's Vestry Hall, 2 Church Entry, London EC4V 5HB. 020 7236 3934.
www.ancientmonumentssociety.org

Church Monuments Society: Contact Dr Sophie Oosterwijk, 34 Bridge St, Shepshed, Leicestershire LE12 9AD.
www.churchmonumentssociety.org

Church Tourism Association: Arthur Rank Centre, Stoneleigh Park, Stoneleigh, Warwickshire CV8 2LZ. Secretary: Rosemary Watts: 01522 731281. http://churchtourismassociation.info.
Email: chrchtours@aol.com.

Churches Conservation Trust: 1 West Smithfield, London EC1A 9EE. 020 7213 0660. www.visitchurches.org.uk

Churches Tourism Wales: 01792 474447.
www.ctnw.co.uk. Email: Johnw@ctnw.fsnet.co.uk

Council for the Care of Churches: Church House, Great Smith Street, London SW1P 3NZ. 020 7898 1887.
www.churchcare.co.uk. Email: Enquiries@c-of-e.org.uk

Ecclesiological Society: 143 Leathwaite Road, London SW11 6RW.
www.ecclsoc.org

English Heritage: Fortress House, 25 Savile Row, London W1X 2BT. 020 7973 3000. www.english-heritage.org.uk

Friends of Friendless Churches: St Ann's Vestry Hall, 2 Church Entry, London EC4V 5HB. 020 7236 3934.
www.friendsoffriendlesschurches.co.uk

Historic Churches Preservation Trust: 31 Newbury St, EC1A 7HU. 020 7600 6090. www.historicchurches.org.uk

Mausolea and Monuments Trust: 70 Cowcross St, London EC1M 6EJ. 020 7608 1441.
www. Mausolea-monuments.org.uk

The Monumental Brass Society: Lowe Hill House, Stratford St Mary, Suffolk CO7 6JX. 01206 337239.
www.mbs-brasses.co.uk. Email: martin@hmstuchfield.co.uk

National Association of Decorative and Fine Arts: (NADFAS): 8, Guildford Street, London WC1N 1DA. 020 7430 0730.
www.nadfas.org.uk

North-west Multi-Faith Tourism Association: The Parish Office, Church Road, Thornton Hough, Wirral CH63 1JP. 0151 336 1654. Email: Allsaints@eidosnet.co.uk

Open Churches Trust: c/o The Really Useful Group, 22 Tower St, London WC2H 9TW. 020 7240 0880.
www.openchurchestrust.org.uk

Round Tower Churches Society: Crabbe Hall, Burnham Market, King's Lynn, Norfolk PE31 8EN. 01328 738237.
www.roundtowers.org.uk

Scotland's Churches Scheme: Dunedin, Holehouse Road, Eaglesham, Glasgow G76 OJF 01355 302416.
Email: fraser@dunedin767.freeserve.co.uk.

The Stained Glass Museum: The Cathedral, Ely, Cambridgeshire CB7 4DN. 01353 660347.

Welsh Historic Environment Agency (CADW): Crown Building, Cathays Park, Cardiff CF10 3NQ. 029 2050 0200.
www.CADW.wales.gov.uk

Churchyards

British Sundial Society: 4 New Wokingham Road, Crowthorne, Berkshire RG45 7NR. 01344 772303.

Caring for God's Acre: 6 West Street, Leominster HR6 8ES. 01568 11154. www.caringforgod'sacre.co.uk

The Living Churchyard and Cemetery Project: The Arthur Rank Centre, Stoneleigh Park, Warwickshire CV8 2LZ. 02476 853060.

Memorials by Artists: Snape Priory, Saxmundham, Suffolk IP17 1SA. 01728 688934. www.memorialsbyartists.co.uk

National Monuments Record: Kemble Drive, Swindon N2 2GZ. 01793 414600. www.english-heritage.org.uk

Appendix 4

Further Reading

Church exploring is a vast subject. If you have realized as much from a cursory read of this book and got this far, then you are already probably quite an enthusiastic church explorer. In this case you will probably wish to pursue your interest in the subject, so this section might prove useful.

Your best tool for further information is probably the Internet. Even the tiniest communities often gain a mention on websites nowadays. The Web will guide you to relevant libraries and other sources of information, and quite probably other church explorers with similar interests.

Another major source is the Victoria County History (VCH). Although this mammoth publishing task has been in progress for 105 years, the ultimate object of producing an exhaustive local history of every community in England is far from complete. Check on www.englandpast.net to find out the state of research on the churches in the counties in which you are interested. Your local library should be of help. The VCH is particularly strong on churches.

Church guidebooks should never be forgotten. However, they vary enormously. They are usually hardly in the same league as the VCH in the quality of their research. The main problem with them is that they are often reproduced and slightly altered and amended every few years, but unless more research is done the basic information on the church building in them remains the same. This means that it is very easy to perpetuate mistakes and pass on wrong information. Like a number of other sources they therefore have to be used with caution. Nevertheless, they are often well designed and highly readable, and many dedicated amateur historians have put thousands of hours of work into their creation.

Secondhand bookshops often contain volumes on various aspects of church exploring. The Antiquarian Booksellers Association can be reached on www.aba.org.uk.

If there is a particular secondhand volume you are looking for, websites such as www.abebooks.co.uk, www.bookfinder.co.uk and www.ebay.co.uk might be of help.

Never forget the compendious and hugely influential Pevsner Architectural Guides. The series was started by the late Sir Nikolaus Pevsner in 1951. For more details consult www.pevsner.co.uk or the publisher, Yale University Press. They have a UK website: www.yale-books.co.uk.

Another excellent series comes from Shire Publications of Princes Risborough, Buckinghamshire HP17 9AJ (01844 344301). In their huge and inexpensive range there are books on bellringing, fonts, church monuments, church architecture, misericords, cathedrals and abbeys and many other topics of interest to the church explorer. They also have a volume on epitaphs, a subject not covered in this book, and a title called *Discovering Famous Graves*, a topic which is likewise not covered in this book. Two other books on the latter subject you might find useful are listed below. The Shire website, www.Shirebooks.co.uk, contains details of all their titles in print.

Another publisher that church explorers should know about is Folly Publications, a very small business based at 151 West Malvern Road, Malvern, Worcestershire WR14 4AY (01684 565211). This publisher produces a series of small inexpensive guides to historic churches in 14 English counties and also much of Wales. Their website is www.follypublications.co.uk.

Other books that provide good general reading on parish churches are listed in the Bibliography. In addition, the following titles might prove useful.

Betjeman, J. with Hogarth, P. *In Praise of Churches*, John Murray, London, 1996

Bettey, J. *Church and Parish*, Batsford, London, 1987

Bowen, D. *Looking at Churches*, David and Charles, Newton Abbot, 1976

Braun, H. *Parish Churches*, Faber, London, 1970

Burman, P. *The Churchyards Handbook*, CHP, London, 1988

Chapman, L. *Church Memorial Brasses and Brass Rubbing*, Shire, Princes Risborough, 1987

Clarke, B. and Betjeman, J. *English Churches*, Studio Vista, London, 1964

Clifton-Taylor, A. *English Parish Churches as Works of Art*, Oxford University Press, London, 1974

Cole, T. *Scratch Dials* (self-published), Saxmundham, 1934

Cunnington, P. *How Old Is That Church?* Marston House, Yeovil, 1990

Duffy, E. *The Stripping of the Altars*, Yale University Press, New Haven and London, 1992

Duffy, E. *The Voices of Morebath: Reformation and Rebellion in an English Village*, Yale University Press, London, 2001

Fewins, C. *Be a Church Detective*, Canterbury Press, Norwich, 2005

Friar, S. *The Local History Companion*, Sutton, Stroud, 2001

Goode, W. *Round Tower Churches of South East England*, Round Tower Churches Society, Burnham Market, 1994

Greenwood, D. *Who's Buried Where in England*, Constable, London, 1990

Harbison, R. *The Shell Guide to English Parish Churches*, Deutsch, London, 1992

Hayman, R. *Church Misericords and Bench Ends*, Shire, Princes Risborough, 1989

Hey, D. *Oxford Dictionary of Local and Family History*, Oxford University Press, Oxford, 1997

Hoskins, W. *The Making of the English Landscape*, Hodder and Stoughton, London, 1955.

Kerrigan, M. *Who Lies Where? A Guide to Famous Graves*, Fourth Estate, London, 1995

Laird, M. *English Misericords*, John Murray, London, 1986

Morris, R. *Churches in the Landscape*, Dent, London, 1989

Richardson, J. *The Local Historian's Encyclopaedia*, Historical Publications, New Barnet, 1986

Sinden, D. *The English Country Church*, Sidgwick and Jackson, London, 1988

Smith, E., Cook, O. and Hutton, G. *English Parish Churches*, Thames and Hudson, London, 1952–

Tate, W. *The Parish Chest*, Phillimore, Chichester, 1983

Timpson, J. *Timpson's Country Churches*, Weidenfeld and Nicolson, London, 1998

Wright, G. *Discovering Epitaphs*, Shire, Princes Risborough, 1972

Appendix 5

Glossary

Abbey Ecclesiastical establishment occupied by monks or nuns under an abbot or abbess or a church that once belonged to such an establishment.

Aisle The part of the church on either side of the nave, usually separated from the nave by a row of pillars.

Altar Flat-topped table of stone or wood for the celebration of the Mass, or Eucharist.

Anchorite's cell Small dwelling for the solitary confinement of a pious recluse, often built against the north wall of the church.

Apse Semi-circular or polygonal end to the chancel. Often has an arched or domed roof.

Arcade Series of columns or pillars supporting arches.

Aumbry Small cupboard or recess, in a wall near the altar, to house the sacred vessels used at Mass or Communion.

Beak head Form of decoration common in Norman architecture. The stylized head of a bird or animal with a long beak is used as a repeated sculptural motif to achieve an ornamental effect round doorways or arches.

Belfry Part of the church tower, turret, or a detached building which contains the bells.

Bellcote Small tower or arch which contains bells.

Bench Early form of seating: traditionally moveable and used by the congregation in the nave of the church.

Bench end Vertical sections at each end of a bench. Medieval examples are often richly carved.

Boss Ornamental projection in stone or timber at the point where the ribs of a vault or roof meet.

Box pew Seating surrounded by a panelled wooden enclosure with a door.

Brass A memorial tablet of brass, with figure or inscription, set either in the floor or on the wall of a church.

Buttress Mass of masonry built against a wall to give extra stability or counteract the outward thrust of an arch or vault behind the wall.

Capital Topmost part (often decorated) of a column or pillar.

Cemetery A place set aside for the burial of the dead, not necessarily attached to a church.

Chancel The area of the main body of the church east of the nave and transepts.

Chantry Either an endowment – a sum of money laid aside – for the maintenance of one or more priests to say Masses for the souls of departed benefactors, or the chapel, altar or part of the church endowed for the same purpose.

Chapel Any building or part of a building used for worship that is not a church.

Charnel house Crypt or vault in which bones were piled when removed from graves in the churchyard.

Churchyard The enclosed piece of ground in which a church stands.

Choir The part of a church occupied by those who sing the services, usually at the east end.

Clerestorey (Clearstory) Upper storey of the nave walls pierced by windows rising above the roofs of the aisles.

College A college of canons is a group of non-monastic clergy who hold services in a church which receives special funds for the maintenance of their life of prayer. In medieval times the object of the foundation was generally to pray for the souls of the founders of the college.

Column A round pillar, with base, shaft and capital.

Communion table In Elizabethan and Jacobean times the medieval altar was replaced by a wooden table. The table was originally placed in the centre of the chancel, away from the east wall, and was often handsomely carved.

Consecration cross A series of crosses, usually 12, marked on the inside and outside walls to be blessed by the bishop and anointed with holy oil during the consecration of the church.

Corbel A projection of wood or stone jutting out from a wall and designed to support a beam.

Crypt A vaulted underground chamber, originally marking the grave of a holy person or for the storage or veneration of relics.

Dissolution Term used to describe the disbanding of the monasteries and appropriation of their lands by King Henry VIII.

Doom A wall painting that is a dramatic representation of the Last Judgement, usually painted above the chancel arch.

Easter sepulchre Recess in chancel wall used to house the consecrated host from Maundy Thursday until Easter Morning. Symbolic of Christ's entombment.

Fan vaulting The most spectacular form of Gothic vaulting (see *Vault*).

Flying buttress Buttress in the form of an open half-arch, which directs the thrust of a high wall across the roof of an aisle to a main buttress on the outer wall.

Font Receptacle for the holy water used in baptism.

Gable The triangular upper section of an exterior wall at the end of a roof.

Gargoyle A projecting water spout, with sculptured human or animal shape, used to throw water clear of a wall.

Green Man A potent symbol of pagan mythology in the form of a head of a man peering from foliage. Symbolizes creative fertility in nature.

Grisaille Clear glass which is painted in geometric patterns and with leaf decoration within those patterns. It cuts out glare but admits more light than stained glass.

Groin The line where two vaults meet.

Grotesque A decorative motif in the form of a comically distorted visage.

Hammer beam A type of roof in which beams project from the side walls but do not cross the roof space as tiebeams do. Instead they carry posts or struts which support the rafters. There may be one or two tiers of hammer beams.

Hatchment A diamond-shaped board bearing a shield of arms, placed in a church after a funeral.

Lancet Tall, narrow and pointed window of the Early English period.

Long-and-short work Characteristic feature of Saxon exterior wall construction used to strengthen the corners of a building.

Lychgate Roofed gateway into the churchyard to shelter the coffin until the arrival of the priest. It originally provided shelter for shrouded bodies at a time when coffins were not common.

Mason's mark Distinguishing mark incised on a piece of stone as a 'signature' to identify the craftsman who worked it.

Mass dial or **Scratch dial** Sundial with radiating lines to indicate the times of church services, scratched or carved on a door jamb or buttress on the south side of the church.

Misericord The projection on the hinged underside of a choir stall, often richly carved, designed to give support to those who found it difficult to stand for long periods during worship.

Nave The body of a church excluding the chancel.

Parclose Screen separating a chapel or aisle from the rest of the church.

Pew An enclosed bench, fixed in its position.

Pier Another word for a pillar (see below) or the masonry from which an arch springs.

Pillar A free-standing vertical structure of stone or wood, slender in proportion relative to its height, which acts as a support to an arch.

Piscina A stone basin usually set in a niche in the wall of the sanctuary. Used to carry away the water with which the priest washes his hands at the Eucharist.

Prayer Book Churches A phrase used to describe those churches where the furnishings and layout still embody the great shift in emphasis in church worship that came first with the Reformation and later with the Puritans.

Pulpit Platform from which the priest preaches, its decoration reflecting the period in which it was constructed.

Quire Alternative spelling of choir.

Quoin Large dressed cornerstone as it forms the external angle at the meeting of two wall surfaces.

Rib A slender stone support, usually curved, for the infilling of a ceiling.

Rood Cross bearing the body of Christ, flanked by the figures of the Virgin and St John the Evangelist.

Rood screen Carved wooden or stone screen across the chancel which supported the rood loft, a gallery for the Rood, and from which the Gospel was sometimes sung during Mass.

Sanctuary The area of the church containing the principal altar.

Screen A partition of wood, stone or metal dividing one part of a church from another, particularly the choir from the nave.

Sedilia Stone seats for the priests in the south wall of the chancel.

Shrine Originally a container holding the relics of saints. Now commonly used to refer to sacred images kept in a church or to any holy place that is associated with pilgrimages.

Sounding board (also **tester**) A flat, horizontal wooden canopy above a pulpit, designed to amplify and direct a preacher's voice.

Spire A tapering structure in the form of a tall cone or pyramid rising above the tower of a church.

Squint or **hagioscope** An opening cut obliquely in a wall or pillar to give a view of the high altar from side chapels and aisles.

Stall A fixed seat for clergy or others on both sides of the choir of a cathedral or large church.

Steeple A tower surmounted by a spire.

Stoup A receptacle for holy water, usually placed near the entrance to a church, with which worshippers may sprinkle themselves.

Tester Canopy over a pulpit, altar or shrine.

Tracery Intersecting decorative ribwork in the upper parts of Gothic windows.

Transept The transverse arm of a church.

Tympanum Area between the lintel of a doorway and the arch above it. Often filled with sculpture.

Vault An arched stone ceiling.

Votive cross A small rudimentary cross scratched in stonework, often near a church entrance, to commemorate the making of a vow.

Appendix 6

Bibliography

Betjeman, J. *Collins Guide to English Parish Churches*, Collins, London, 1958

Bradley, S. and Pevsner, N. *London: The City Churches*, Penguin, London, 1998

Caiger-Smith, A. *English Medieval Mural Paintings*, Oxford University Press, Oxford, 1963

Camp, J. *Bells and Bellringing*, Shire, Princes Risborough, 1968

Chatfield, M. *Churches the Victorians Forgot*, Moorland, Ashbourne, 1989

Child, Mark *Discovering Church Architecture*, Shire, Princes Risborough, 1976

Child, Mark *Discovering Churchyards*, Shire, Princes Risborough, 1982

Cook, G. *The English Medieval Parish Church*, Phoenix House, London, 1954

Cowen, P. *Stained Glass in Britain*, Michael Joseph, London, 1985

Cox, J. *The Parish Churches of England*, Batsford, London, 1935

Daniel, C. *Sundials*, Shire, Princes Risborough, 2004

Delderfield, E. *A Guide to Church Furniture*, David and Charles, Newton Abbott, 1966

Ford, E. and Haywood, J. *Church Treasures in the Oxford District*, Alan Sutton, Gloucester, 1984

Foster, R. *Discovering English Churches*, BBC, London, 1981

Friar, S. *The Sutton Companion to Churches*, Sutton, Stroud, 1996

Harries, J. *Discovering Churches*, Shire, Princes Risborough, 1972

Harries, J. *Discovering Stained Glass*, Shire, Princes Risborough, 1968

Howkins, C. *Discovering Church Furniture*, Shire, Princes Risborough, 1969

Humphrey, S. ed. *Churches and Chapels of Northern England*, A&C Black (Blue Guide), London, 1991

Jenkins, S. *England's Thousand Best Churches*, Penguin, London, 1999

Jones, L. *The Beauty of English Churches*, Constable, London, 1978

Jones, L. *The Observer's Book of Old English Churches*, Warne, London, 1965

Jones, L. with Tricker, R. *County Guide to English Churches*, Countryside, Newbury, 1992

Kemp, B. *Church Monuments*, Shire, Princes Risborough, 1985

Lees, H. *English Churchyard Memorials*, Tempus, Stroud, 2000

Leonard, J. *London's Parish Churches*, Breedon Books, Derby, 1997

Meakin, T. *A Basic Church Dictionary*, SCM-Canterbury Press, Norwich, 1990

Paul, N. *Enjoying Old Parish Churches*, Pentland Press, Edinburgh, 1996

Pevsner, N. *The Buildings of England*, Penguin, London, 1951

Rouse, E. *Medieval Wall Paintings*, Shire, Princes Risborough, 1968

Salter, M. *The Old Parish Churches of Devon*, Folly Publications, Malvern, 1999

Shreeve, S. and Stilgoe, L. *The Round Tower Churches of Norfolk*, SCM-Canterbury Press, Norwich, 2001

Slader, J. *The Churches of Devon*, David and Charles, Newton Abbot, 1968

Soden, R. *A Guide to Welsh Parish Churches*, Gomer Press, Llandysul, 1984

Vale, E. *Churches*, Batsford, London, 1954

Vayne, S. *Nicholson's Guide to English Churches*, Robert Nicholson, London, 1984

Verey, D. *Cotswold Churches*, Alan Sutton, Gloucester, 1982

Vigar, J. *Exploring Sussex Churches*, Meresborough Books, Gillingham, 1985

Vigar, J. *Kent Churches*, Dovecote Press, Wimborne, 2001

Whitelaw, J. *Hertfordshire Churches*, Oldcastle Books, Harpenden, 1990

Index of Church Names and Places

Dauntsey (Wiltshire) 182
Daventry (Northamptonshire) 266
Dean Prior (Devon) 171
Dearham (Cumbria) 35, 219
Dedham (Essex) 257
Deerhurst (Gloucestershire) 37illus.,
    99, 99illus., 168, 207, 257
Delamere (Cheshire) 216
Denbigh (Denbighshire) 277
Denchworth (Oxfordshire) 208
Denham (Buckinghamshire) 207
Dennington (Suffolk) 36, 47, 51,
    106illus., 107, 109, 141illus., 145,
    148, 271
Deptford (Greater London) 264
Derby (Derbyshire) 254
Derwen (Denbighshire) 145
Devizes (Wiltshire) 148, 273
Dewsbury (West Yorkshire) 169
Didling (West Sussex) 107, 272
Didmarton (Gloucestershire) 221
Digswell (Hertfordshire) 208
Dilwyn (Herefordshire) 259
Disley (Cheshire) 33
Dittisham (Devon) 115, 144
Doddiscombsleigh (Devon) 169, 171
Dodford (Worcestershire) 274
Dolton (Devon) 99
Dolwyddelan (Conwy) 132
Doncaster (South Yorkshire) 276
Donnington (Herefordshire) 34
Dorchester (Oxfordshire) 102, 168,
    169, 171, 208, 268
Dormington (Herefordshire) 47, 51
Doveridge (Derbyshire) 218
Downton (Wiltshire) 223
Draycot Cerne (Wiltshire) 208
Drayton Beauchamp
    (Buckinghamshire) 169, 207
Driffield (East Riding of Yorkshire) 36
Dronfield (Derbyshire) 134
Duloe (Cornwall) 196
Dulwich (Greater London) 264
Dummer (Hampshire) 258
Dundee 248
Dunsfold (Surrey) 107, 271
Dunstable (Bedfordshire) 196, 250
Dunster (Somerset) 145, 269
Duntisbourne Abbots
    (Gloucestershire) 222
Duntisbourne Rouse (Gloucestershire)
    3illus., 126, 181, 258
Dunton Bassett (Leicestershire) 107
Durham 47illus., 256

Durham Cathedral 47illus.
Duxford St John (Cambridgeshire) 251
Dymock (Gloucestershire) 34, 258
Dyrham (Gloucestershire) 8, 207

Ealing (Greater London) 265
Eardisley (Herefordshire) 97illus.,
    100, 259
Earl Soham (Suffolk) 36
Earl Stonham (Suffolk) 136, 271
Earls Barton (Northamptonshire) 72,
    74, 266
Easby (North Yorkshire) 182
East Allington (Devon) 115
East Bergholt (Suffolk) 66
East Brent (Somerset) 36
East Budleigh (Devon) 107, 196
East Dean (East Sussex) 36
East Dereham (Norfolk) 66, 208, 265
East Garston (Berkshire) 33
East Harling (Norfolk) 162illus., 169,
    197, 208, 265
East Hendred (Oxfordshire) 214
East Horndon (Essex) 148, 257
East Horsley (Surrey) 208
East Leake (Nottinghamshire) 138
East Markham (Nottinghamshire)
    208, 267
East Meon (Hampshire) 74, 223, 258
East Portlemouth (Devon) 144
East Shefford (Berkshire) 196, 250
East Sutton (Kent) 208
East Wellow (Hampshire) 181, 258
Eastbourne (East Sussex), St Mary 171
Eastleach (Gloucestershire) 35
Eastleach Turville (Gloucestershire) 35
Eastnor (Herefordshire) 197
Eastry (Kent) 34
Eastwood Great Bardfield (Essex) 51
Eaton (Leicestershire) 216
Eaton Bishop (Herefordshire) 168
Eaton Bray (Bedfordshire) 101, 250
Eccles (Greater Manchester) 261
Ecclesfield (South Yorkshire) 276
Eccleston (Cheshire) 252
Eckington (Derbyshire) 34
Eckington (Worcestershire) 107
Edenfield (Lancashire) 34
Edenhall (Cumbria) 207
Edensor (Derbyshire) 254
Edinburgh 248
Edington (Wiltshire) 41, 198, 273
Edlesborough (Buckinghamshire) 11,
    196, 213, 216, 251

Ingham (Norfolk) 57, 265
Ingleby Arncliffe (North Yorkshire) 8
Inglesham (Wiltshire) 36, 273
Ingrave (Essex) 257
Inkberrow (Worcestershire) 35
Instow (Devon) 100
Iona Abbey 248
Ipplepen (Devon) 115
Ipswich (Suffolk) 51, 271
Ireton (Cumbria) 219
Iron Acton (Gloucestershire) 221
Irthlingborough (Northamptonshire) 66
Isel (Cumbria) 35
Isle Abbotts (Somerset) 270
Isleham (Cambridgeshire) 207, 251
Isleworth (Greater London) 34
The Italian Chapel, Orkney 248
Itchingfield (West Sussex) 226
Ivinghoe (Buckinghamshire) 251
Ivychurch (Kent) 261
Ixworth Thorpe (Suffolk) 44

Jacobstowe (Devon) 100
Jarrow (Tyne & Wear) 256

Kedington (Suffolk) 109, 198, 271
Kedleston (Derbyshire) 8, 35, 254
Kelham (Nottinghamshire) 8
Kelling (Norfolk) 131
Kelmscott (Oxfordshire) 268
Kempley (Gloucestershire) 88, 175, 181, 182, 183, 258
Kempsey (Worcestershire) 169
Kempsford (Gloucestershire) 8, 55illus., 136, 258
Kemsing (Kent) 209
Kenardington (Kent) 35
Kendal (Cumbria) 254
Kenley (Shropshire) 216
Kenn (Devon) 100
Kensington (Greater London) 263
Kenton (Devon) 115
Kenwyn (Cornwall) 223
Kersey (Suffolk) 271
Ketteringham (Norfolk) 35
Kettlebaston (Suffolk) 100
Ketton (Rutland) 268
Kew Green (Greater London) 197, 264
Keyston (Cambridgeshire) 78illus.
Kidderminster (Worcestershire) 208
Kidlington (Oxfordshire) 268
Kidwelly (Carmarthenshire) 38, 278

Kilburn (Greater London) 263
Kilkhampton (Cornwall) 107, 196, 214, 253
Kilpeck (Herefordshire) 29–30, 49illus., 73illus., 259
Kimpton (Hertfordshire) 260
King Charles the Martyr (Tunbridge Wells, Kent) 34, 261
King's Bromley (Staffordshire) 36
King's Lynn (Norfolk) 39, 57, 208, 265
King's Norton (Leicestershire) 262
King's Sombourne (Hampshire) 207
King's Sutton (Northamptonshire) 194, 198
Kingsdown (Kent) 261
Kingsthorpe (Northamptonshire) 134
Kingston on Soar (Nottinghamshire) 267
Kington St Michael (Wiltshire) 222illus.
Kinlet (Shropshire) 269
Kinnersley (Herefordshire) 197
Kinver (Staffordshire) 270
Kirk Hammerton (North Yorkshire) 275
Kirk Langley (Derbyshire) 144
Kirkburn (East Riding of Yorkshire) 100
Kirkby Lonsdale (Cumbria) 254
Kirkby Malham (North Yorkshire) 108illus., 109
Kirkby Malzeard (North Yorkshire) 36
Kirkby Stephen (Cumbria) 219
Kirkdale (North Yorkshire) 31, 33, 275
Kirkheaton (West Yorkshire) 198
Kirknewton (Northumberland) 267
Kirkoswald (Cumbria) 66
Kirkstead (Lincolnshire) 263
Knaresborough (North Yorkshire) 35, 275
Knebworth (Hertfordshire) 8, 197, 208, 260
Knowlton (Dorset) 5illus., 11, 213, 214
Knowlton (Kent) 8

Lackford (Suffolk) 101illus.
Lacock (Wiltshire) 273
Lambeth (Greater London) 264
Lambourn (Berkshire) 250
Lambourne (Essex) 170

Index of Subjects

62, 79, 289
Perpendicular period 79–80

capitals 172, 288
Decorated period 78illus.
Caring for God's Acre 229
cartouche tablets 191
carvings
ballflower decoration 50
beakhead ornament 52, 53illus., 73, 287
dog tooth ornament 50
as indication of the age of a church 36–8
poppy heads 106illus., 107, 110
cast iron, use for gravestones 236
Catherine of Aragon 80
Celts
Celtic crosses 219
church designs 14
veneration of yew trees 218
cemeteries 223–4, 288
see also churchyards
chained books 134
chancels 11, 12illus., 123, 288
arches, wall paintings 180
chancel screens 140
'off a cog' orientation 19
seating 110–12
skew chancels 19
change-ringing 139
chantry chapels 12illus., 31, 57, 147–8, 288
chapels 288
Charles II (King of England) 210
charnel houses (bone holes) 126–7, 226, 288
Chaucer, Geoffrey, *Canterbury Tales* 122
chests 131–2
choirs (quires) 138, 288
Christianity, origins in Britain 70
Christopher, St 177, 178illus.
church architecture, development 69–88
Church Building Act (1818) 86
church houses 226
Church Monuments Society 186
church tourism officers 245
churches
access to 243–7
age 21–9
as indicated by carvings 36–8
as shown by corbels 29–30

as shown by sundials 31–6
as shown by windows 23–9
cruciform churches 97
dedication 19–21
designs 11–13
interiors 91–139
orientation 18–19
settings 3–11
hilltops 10illus., 11
timber-framed churches 56illus.
Churches Conservation Trust 9
churchyards 213–40, 226–8, 288
activities in 215
arrow sharpening 38
buildings within 226
circular churchyards 64, 213–14
crosses within 218–21, 234illus.
having two churches 214
as nature reserves 229–31
on prehistoric sites 214
yew trees in 216–18
see also cemeteries
'Churchyards' (Betjeman) 229
Civil War 5, 82
Classical period
architectural developments 83–4
pulpits 114illus.
reredoses 123illus.
screens 143illus.
windows 28–9
clerestories (clearstories) 22, 288
coffin stones 222illus.
colleges 288
columns 172, 288
Early English period 76
see also pillars
Communion Tables 288
Comper, Sir J. Ninian 88
confessios 120
consecration crosses 40, 135, 289
Contrasts (Pugin) 86
corbels 29–30, 30illus., 151, 288
see also roofs
crants (maiden's garlands, virgin's crowns) 136
crockets 62
Cromwell, Oliver 82
crosses, within churchyards 218–21, 234illus.
'cruciform' churches 11
crypts 124–9, 289

Decorated period
architectural developments 76–9